# PEARLS OF BOUNTY

# PEARLS OF BOUNTY

*Selections from the Prayers,*
*Tablets, and Talks of 'Abdu'l-Bahá*

BAHÁ'Í
PUBLISHING
WILMETTE, ILLINOIS

Bahá'í Publishing

401 Greenleaf Avenue, Wilmette, Illinois 60091

Copyright © 2021 by the National Spiritual Assembly
of the Bahá'ís of the United States

All rights reserved. Published 2021

Printed in the United States of America on acid-free
paper ∞

ISBN 978-1-61851-191-1

24  23  22  21     4  3  2  1

Cover design by Carlos Esparza
Book design by Patrick Falso

# Contents

# CONTENTS

# Preface

This volume provides a selection of prayers, Tablets, and excerpts from Tablets by 'Abdu'l-Bahá, as well as the text of twelve table talks He gave in 'Akká. They have been chosen from material that has been translated into English and prepared for publication over the years in the course of the work at the Bahá'í World Centre and been made available on the Bahá'í Reference Library.

Part 1 includes nineteen prayers, most of which were revealed for or about children. The twenty-eight Tablets in Part 2 cover a wide range of subjects. Foremost among these Tablets are 'Abdu'l-Bahá's first and second Tablets to The Hague, letters written to the members of the Executive Committee of the Central Organization for a Durable Peace in 1919 and 1920. Parts of the English translation of the first Tablet to The Hague were originally published in the volume *Selections from the Writings of 'Abdu'l-Bahá*, but the Tablet is included here in its entirety. The second Tablet to The Hague is newly translated.

Also included in Part 2 are a Tablet the latter part of which was recorded in 'Abdu'l-Bahá's own voice and is played for Bahá'í pilgrims during their visit to the House of the Master in Haifa, and a Tablet describing the operation of the village storehouse, which is to provide services to the community including education, public health, and support for the poor and needy.

Part 3 consists of twelve table talks given by 'Abdu'l-Bahá in 'Akká. These talks provide the record of the answers He gave to questions from pilgrims on a variety of spiritual subjects and include accounts about Ṭáhirih and the Conference of Badasht, Shaykh Aḥmad and Siyyid Káẓim, and the Declaration of Bahá'u'lláh.

# 1

# Prayers

# 1

*O Lord!*

Plant this tender seedling in the garden of Thy 1
manifold bounties, water it from the fountains of
Thy loving-kindness and grant that it may grow into
a goodly plant through the outpourings of Thy favor
and grace.

Thou art the Mighty and the Powerful. 2

# 2

*He is the Most Glorious!*

1   O my merciful Lord! This is a hyacinth which hath grown in the garden of Thy good pleasure and a twig which hath appeared in the orchard of true knowledge. Cause it, O Lord of bounty, to be refreshed continually and at all times through Thy vitalizing breezes, and make it verdant, fresh and flourishing through the outpourings of the clouds of Thy favors, O Thou kind Lord!

2   Verily Thou art the All-Glorious.

# 3

*He is God!*

O Thou kind Lord! We are poor children, needy 1
and insignificant, yet we are plants which have
sprouted by Thy heavenly stream and saplings bursting
into bloom in Thy divine springtime. Make us fresh
and verdant by the outpourings of the clouds of Thy
mercy; help us to grow and develop through the rays of
the sun of Thy goodly gifts and cause us to be refreshed
by the quickening breeze wafting from the meadows
of Truth. Grant that we may become flourishing trees
laden with fruit in the orchard of knowledge, brilliant
stars shining above the horizon of eternal happiness and
radiant lamps shedding light upon the assemblage of
mankind.

O Lord! Should Thy tender care be vouchsafed unto 2
us, each one of us would, even as an eagle, soar to the
pinnacle of knowledge, but were we left to ourselves we

would be consumed away and would fall into loss and frustration. Whatever we are, from Thee do we proceed and before Thy threshold do we seek refuge.

3        Thou art the Bestower, the Bountiful, the All-Loving.

# 4

*He is God!*

O Thou pure God! Let these saplings which have 1 sprouted by the stream of Thy guidance become fresh and verdant through the outpourings of the clouds of Thy tender mercy; cause them to be stirred by the gentle winds wafting from the meads of Thy oneness and suffer them to be revived through the rays of the Sun of Reality, that they may continually grow and flourish, and burst into blossoms and fruit.

O Lord God! Bestow upon each one understanding; 2 give them power and strength and cause them to mirror forth Thy divine aid and confirmation, so that they may become highly distinguished among the people.

Thou art the Mighty and the Powerful. 3

# 5

*O Lord!*

1 Help this daughter of the Kingdom to be exalted in both worlds; cause her to turn away from this mortal world of dust and from those who have set their hearts thereon and enable her to have communion and close association with the world of immortality. Give her heavenly power and strengthen her through the breaths of the Holy Spirit that she may arise to serve Thee.

2 Thou art the Mighty One.

# 6

*O Thou kind Lord!*

Grant that these trees may become the adornment 1
of the Abhá Paradise. Cause them to grow through
Thy celestial bounty. Make them fresh and verdant and
besprinkle them with heavenly dewdrops. Attire them
with robes of radiant beauty and crown their heads
with gorgeous blossoms. Adorn them with goodly fruit
and waft over them Thy sweet savors.

Thou art the Bestower, the All-Loving, the Most 2
Radiant, the Most Resplendent.

# 7

*He is God!*

1 O God, my God! We are children who have sucked the milk of divine knowledge from the breast of Thy love and have been admitted into Thy Kingdom while of tender age. We implore Thee in the daytime and in the night season saying: O Lord! Make firm our steps in Thy Faith, guard us within the stronghold of Thy protection, nourish us from Thy heavenly table, enable us to become signs of divine guidance and lamps aglow with upright conduct and aid us through the potency of the angels of Thy kingdom, O Thou Who art the Lord of glory and majesty!

2 Verily Thou art the Bestower, the Merciful, the Compassionate.

# 8

*O Thou Lord of wondrous grace!*

Bestow upon us new blessings. Give to us the fresh- 1
ness of the spring. We are saplings which have
been planted by the fingers of Thy bounty and have
been formed out of the water and clay of Thy tender
affection. We thirst for the living waters of Thy favors
and are dependent upon the outpourings of the clouds
of Thy generosity. Abandon not to itself this grove
wherein our hopes aspire, nor withhold therefrom the
showers of Thy loving-kindness. Grant that from the
clouds of Thy mercy may fall copious rain so that the
trees of our lives may bring forth fruit and we may
attain the most cherished desire of our hearts.

# 9

1   O Thou pure God! I am a little child; grant that the breast of Thy loving-kindness be the breast that I cherish; suffer me to be nourished with the honey and the milk of Thy love; rear me in the bosom of Thy knowledge, and bestow upon me nobility and wisdom while I am still a child.

2   O Thou the Self-Sufficing God! Make me a confidant of the Kingdom of the Unseen. Verily, Thou art the Mighty, the Powerful.

# 10

O Lord! Guard Thou the children that are born in 1
Thy day, are nurtured at the breast of Thy love,
and fostered in the bosom of Thy grace.

O Lord, they are verily young branches growing in 2
the gardens of Thy knowledge, they are boughs bud-
ding in Thy groves of grace. Grant them a share of Thy
generous gifts, make them to thrive and flourish in the
rain that raineth from the clouds of Thy bestowal.

Thou art verily the Generous, the Clement, the 3
Compassionate!

# 11

1   O God! Grant Thy favor, and bestow Thy blessing. Vouchsafe Thy grace, and give a portion of Thy bounty. Enable these men to witness during this year the fulfilment of their hopes. Send down Thy heavenly rain, and provide Thy plenteousness and abundance. Thou art the Powerful, the Mighty.

# 12

*He is God!*

O peerless Lord! Praised be Thou for having kin- 1
dled that light in the glass of the Concourse on
high, for having guided that bird of faithfulness to the
nest of the Abhá Kingdom. Thou hast joined that precious river to the mighty sea, Thou hast returned that
spreading ray of light to the Sun of Truth. Thou hast
welcomed that captive of remoteness into the garden of
reunion, and led him who longed to look upon Thee to
Thy presence in Thy bright place of lights.

Thou art the Lord of tender love, Thou art the last 2
goal of the yearning heart, Thou art the dearest wish of
the martyr's soul.

# 13

1   O my God, O my God! Verily this plant hath yielded its fruit and standeth upright upon its stalk. Verily it hath astounded the farmers and perturbed the envious. O God, water it with showers from the cloud of Thy favors and cause it to yield great harvests heaped up like unto mighty hills in Thy land. Enlighten the hearts with a ray shining forth from Thy Kingdom of Oneness, illumine the eyes by beholding the signs of Thy grace, and gratify the ears by hearing the melodies of the birds of Thy confirmations singing in Thy heavenly gardens, so that these souls may become like thirsty fish swimming in the pools of Thy guidance and like tawny lions roaming in the forests of Thy bounty. Verily Thou art the Generous, the Merciful, the Glorious and the Bestower.

# 14

O Compassionate God! O Lord of Hosts! Praise be 1 unto Thee that Thou hast preferred these little children over the full-grown and mature, and bestowed upon them Thy special favors. Thou hast guided them. Thou hast been kind to them. Thou hast conferred upon them illumination and spirituality. Grant us Thy confirmation so that, when we grow up, we may engage in service to Thy Kingdom, become the cause of educating others, burn like radiant candles and shine like brilliant stars. Thou art the Giver, the Bestower, the Compassionate.

# 15

1   O Thou beloved of my heart and soul! I have no refuge save Thee. I raise no voice at dawn save in Thy commemoration and praise. Thy love encompasseth me and Thy grace is perfect. My hope is in Thee.

2   O God, give me a new life at every instant and bestow upon me the breaths of the Holy Spirit at every moment, in order that I may remain steadfast in Thy love, attain unto great felicity, perceive the manifest light and be in the state of utmost tranquility and submissiveness.

3   Verily, Thou art the Giver, the Forgiver, the Compassionate.

# 16

O God, my God! Give me to drink from the cup of Thy bestowal and illumine my face with the light of guidance. Make me firm in the path of faithfulness, assist me to be steadfast in Thy mighty Covenant, and suffer me to be numbered with Thy chosen servants. Unlock before my face the doors of abundance, grant me deliverance, and sustain me, through means I cannot reckon, from the treasuries of heaven. Suffer me to turn my face toward the countenance of Thy generosity and to be entirely devoted to Thee, O Thou Who art merciful and compassionate! To those that stand fast and firm in Thy Covenant Thou, verily, art gracious and generous. All praise be to God, the Lord of the worlds!

# 17

1 O my God! O Thou Who endowest every just power and equitable dominion with abiding glory and everlasting might, with permanence and stability, with constancy and honor! Aid Thou by Thy heavenly grace every government that acteth justly towards its subjects and every sovereign authority, derived from Thee, that shieldeth the poor and the weak under the banner of its protection.

2 I beseech Thee, by Thy divine grace and surpassing bounty, to aid this just government, the canopy of whose authority is spread over vast and mighty lands and the evidences of whose justice are apparent in its prosperous and flourishing regions. Assist, O my God, its hosts, raise aloft its ensigns, bestow influence upon its word and its utterance, protect its lands, increase its honor, spread its fame, reveal its signs, and unfurl its banner through Thine all-subduing power and Thy resplendent might in the kingdom of creation.

Thou, verily, aidest whomsoever Thou willest, and 3
Thou, verily, art the Almighty, the Most Powerful.

# 18

*O Thou kind God!*

1   From America, that distant country, we hastened to the Holy Land and directed our steps toward this blessed Spot. We attained unto the two blessed and sacred Thresholds and obtained boundless grace therefrom. We have now come to Mount Carmel, which is Thy sacred garden. Most of the Prophets turned to Thee in prayer upon this holy mountain, communing with Thee in the utmost humility at the midnight hour.

2   O Lord! We are now in this blessed place. We beseech Thine infinite bounties and long for a joyous and tranquil conscience. We desire firmness in the Covenant and seek Thy good-pleasure to our last breath.

3   O Lord! Forgive our sins and bestow upon us Thy manifold favors. Shield us within the shelter of Thy protection. Guard and preserve these two little children and nurture them in the embrace of Thy Love.

Thou art the Forgiver, the Resplendent, the 4 Ever-Loving.

# 19

1   O Thou forgiving God! Forgive the sins of my loving mother, pardon her shortcomings, cast upon her the glance of Thy gracious providence, and enable her to gain admittance into Thy Kingdom.

2   O God! From the earliest days of my life she educated and nurtured me, yet I did not recompense her for her toil and labors. Do Thou reward her by granting her eternal life and making her exalted in Thy Kingdom.

3   Verily, Thou art the Forgiver, the Bestower, and the Kind.

# 2

# Tablets

# Tablets to The Hague

# 1

## First Tablet to The Hague
## 17 December 1919

O ye esteemed ones who are pioneers among the well-wishers of the world of humanity![1]

The letters which ye sent during the war were not received, but a letter dated February 11th, 1916, has just come to hand, and immediately an answer is being written. Your intention deserves a thousand praises, because you are serving the world of humanity, and this is conducive to the happiness and welfare of all. This recent war has proved to the world and the people that war is destruction while universal peace is construction; war is death while peace is life; war is rapacity and bloodthirstiness while peace is beneficence and humaneness;

war is an appurtenance of the world of nature while peace is of the foundation of the religion of God; war is darkness upon darkness while peace is heavenly light; war is the destroyer of the edifice of mankind while peace is the everlasting life of the world of humanity; war is like a devouring wolf while peace is like the angels of heaven; war is the struggle for existence while peace is mutual aid and cooperation among the peoples of the world and the cause of the good pleasure of the True One in the heavenly realm.

3    There is not one soul whose conscience does not testify that in this day there is no more important matter in the world than that of universal peace. Every just one bears witness to this and adores that esteemed Assembly because its aim is that this darkness may be changed into light, this bloodthirstiness into kindness, this torment into bliss, this hardship into ease and this enmity and hatred into fellowship and love. Therefore, the effort of those esteemed souls is worthy of praise and commendation.

4    But the wise souls who are aware of the essential relationships emanating from the realities of things consider that one single matter cannot, by itself, influence the human reality as it ought and should, for until the minds of men become united, no important matter can be accomplished. At present universal peace is a matter of great importance, but unity of conscience is essen-

tial, so that the foundation of this matter may become secure, its establishment firm and its edifice strong.

Therefore Bahá'u'lláh, fifty years ago, expounded 5 this question of universal peace at a time when He was confined in the fortress of 'Akká and was wronged and imprisoned. He wrote about this important matter of universal peace to all the great sovereigns of the world, and established it among His friends in the Orient. The horizon of the East was in utter darkness, nations displayed the utmost hatred and enmity towards each other, religions thirsted for each other's blood, and it was darkness upon darkness. At such a time Bahá'u'lláh shone forth like the sun from the horizon of the east and illumined Persia with the lights of these teachings.

Among His teachings was the declaration of uni- 6 versal peace. People of different nations, religions and sects who followed Him came together to such an extent that remarkable gatherings were instituted consisting of the various nations and religions of the East. Every soul who entered these gatherings saw but one nation, one teaching, one pathway, one order, for the teachings of Bahá'u'lláh were not limited to the establishment of universal peace. They embraced many teachings which supplemented and supported that of universal peace.

Among these teachings was the independent inves- 7 tigation of reality so that the world of humanity may be saved from the darkness of imitation and attain to the truth; may tear off and cast away this ragged and outgrown garment of a thousand years ago and may put on the robe woven in the utmost purity and holiness in the loom of reality. As reality is one and cannot admit of multiplicity, therefore different opinions must ultimately become fused into one.

8    And among the teachings of Bahá'u'lláh is the oneness of the world of humanity; that all human beings are the sheep of God and He is the kind Shepherd. This Shepherd is kind to all the sheep, because He created them all, trained them, provided for them and protected them. There is no doubt that the Shepherd is kind to all the sheep and should there be among these sheep ignorant ones, they must be educated; if there be children, they must be trained until they reach maturity; if there be sick ones, they must be cured. There must be no hatred and enmity, for as by a kind physician these ignorant, sick ones should be treated.

9    And among the teachings of Bahá'u'lláh is that religion must be the cause of fellowship and love. If it becomes the cause of estrangement then it is not needed, for religion is like a remedy; if it aggravates the disease then it becomes unnecessary.

10   And among the teachings of Bahá'u'lláh is that religion must be in conformity with science and reason, so that it may influence the hearts of men. The foundation must be solid and must not consist of imitations.

And among the teachings of Bahá'u'lláh is that 11
religious, racial, political, economic and patriotic
prejudices destroy the edifice of humanity. As long as
these prejudices prevail, the world of humanity will not
have rest. For a period of 6,000 years history informs
us about the world of humanity. During these 6,000
years the world of humanity has not been free from war,
strife, murder and bloodthirstiness. In every period war
has been waged in one country or another and that war
was due to either religious prejudice, racial prejudice,
political prejudice or patriotic prejudice. It has therefore been ascertained and proved that all prejudices are
destructive of the human edifice. As long as these prejudices persist, the struggle for existence must remain
dominant, and bloodthirstiness and rapacity continue.
Therefore, even as was the case in the past, the world
of humanity cannot be saved from the darkness of
nature and cannot attain illumination except through
the abandonment of prejudices and the acquisition of
the morals of the Kingdom.

If this prejudice and enmity are on account of reli- 12
gion consider that religion should be the cause of fellowship, otherwise it is fruitless. And if this prejudice
be the prejudice of nationality consider that all mankind are of one nation; all have sprung from the tree of
Adam, and Adam is the root of the tree. That tree is one
and all these nations are like branches, while the individuals of humanity are like leaves, blossoms and fruits

thereof. Then the establishment of various nations and the consequent shedding of blood and destruction of the edifice of humanity result from human ignorance and selfish motives.

13    As to the patriotic prejudice, this is also due to absolute ignorance, for the surface of the earth is one native land. Every one can live in any spot on the terrestrial globe. Therefore all the world is man's birthplace. These boundaries and outlets have been devised by man. In the creation, such boundaries and outlets were not assigned. Europe is one continent, Asia is one continent, Africa is one continent, Australia is one continent, but some of the souls, from personal motives and selfish interests, have divided each one of these continents and considered a certain part as their own country. God has set up no frontier between France and Germany; they are continuous. Yet, in the first centuries, selfish souls, for the promotion of their own interests, have assigned boundaries and outlets and have, day by day, attached more importance to these, until this led to intense enmity, bloodshed and rapacity in subsequent centuries. In the same way this will continue indefinitely, and if this conception of patriotism remains limited within a certain circle, it will be the primary cause of the world's destruction. No wise and just person will acknowledge these imaginary distinctions. Every limited area which we call our native country we regard as our motherland, whereas the terrestrial globe is the

motherland of all, and not any restricted area. In short, for a few days we live on this earth and eventually we are buried in it, it is our eternal tomb. Is it worth while that we should engage in bloodshed and tear one another to pieces for this eternal tomb? Nay, far from it, neither is God pleased with such conduct nor would any sane man approve of it.

Consider! The blessed animals engage in no patriotic 14 quarrels. They are in the utmost fellowship with one another and live together in harmony. For example, if a dove from the east and a dove from the west, a dove from the north and a dove from the south chance to arrive, at the same time, in one spot, they immediately associate in harmony. So is it with all the blessed animals and birds. But the ferocious animals, as soon as they meet, attack and fight with each other, tear each other to pieces and it is impossible for them to live peaceably together in one spot. They are all unsociable and fierce, savage and combative fighters.

Regarding the economic prejudice, it is apparent that 15 whenever the ties between nations become strengthened and the exchange of commodities accelerated, and any economic principle is established in one country, it will ultimately affect the other countries and universal benefits will result. Then why this prejudice?

As to the political prejudice, the policy of God must 16 be followed and it is indisputable that the policy of God is greater than human policy. We must follow the

Divine policy and that applies alike to all individuals. He treats all individuals alike: no distinction is made, and that is the foundation of the Divine Religions.

17    And among the teachings of Bahá'u'lláh is the origination of one language that may be spread universally among the people. This teaching was revealed from the pen of Bahá'u'lláh in order that this universal language may eliminate misunderstandings from among mankind.

18    And among the teachings of Bahá'u'lláh is the equality of women and men. The world of humanity has two wings—one is women and the other men. Not until both wings are equally developed can the bird fly. Should one wing remain weak, flight is impossible. Not until the world of women becomes equal to the world of men in the acquisition of virtues and perfections, can success and prosperity be attained as they ought to be.

19    And among the teachings of Bahá'u'lláh is voluntary sharing of one's property with others among mankind. This voluntary sharing is greater than equality, and consists in this, that man should not prefer himself to others, but rather should sacrifice his life and property for others. But this should not be introduced by coercion so that it becomes a law and man is compelled to follow it. Nay, rather, man should voluntarily and of his own choice sacrifice his property and life for others, and spend willingly for the poor, just as is done in Persia among the Bahá'ís.

And among the teachings of Bahá'u'lláh is man's 20 freedom, that through the ideal Power he should be free and emancipated from the captivity of the world of nature; for as long as man is captive to nature he is a ferocious animal, as the struggle for existence is one of the exigencies of the world of nature. This matter of the struggle for existence is the fountain-head of all calamities and is the supreme affliction.

And among the teachings of Bahá'u'lláh is that 21 religion is a mighty bulwark. If the edifice of religion shakes and totters, commotion and chaos will ensue and the order of things will be utterly upset, for in the world of mankind there are two safeguards that protect man from wrongdoing. One is the law which punishes the criminal; but the law prevents only the manifest crime and not the concealed sin; whereas the ideal safeguard, namely, the religion of God, prevents both the manifest and the concealed crime, trains man, educates morals, compels the adoption of virtues and is the all-inclusive power which guarantees the felicity of the world of mankind. But by religion is meant that which is ascertained by investigation and not that which is based on mere imitation, the foundations of Divine Religions and not human imitations.

And among the teachings of Bahá'u'lláh is that 22 although material civilization is one of the means for the progress of the world of mankind, yet until it becomes combined with Divine civilization, the desired result, which is the felicity of mankind, will not be attained. Consider! These battleships that reduce a city to ruins within the space of an hour are the result of material civilization; likewise the Krupp guns, the Mauser rifles, dynamite, submarines, torpedo boats, armed aircraft and bombers—all these weapons of war are the malignant fruits of material civilization. Had material civilization been combined with Divine civilization, these fiery weapons would never have been invented. Nay, rather, human energy would have been wholly devoted to useful inventions and would have been concentrated on praiseworthy discoveries. Material civilization is like a lamp-glass. Divine civilization is the lamp itself and the glass without the light is dark. Material civilization is like the body. No matter how infinitely graceful, elegant and beautiful it may be, it is dead. Divine civilization is like the spirit, and the body gets its life from the spirit, otherwise it becomes a corpse. It has thus been made evident that the world of mankind is in need of the breaths of the Holy Spirit. Without the spirit the world of mankind is lifeless, and without this light the world of mankind is in utter darkness. For the world of nature is an animal world. Until man is born again from the world of nature, that is to say, becomes detached from the world of nature, he is essentially an animal, and it is the teachings of God which convert this animal into a human soul.

TABLETS

And among the teachings of Bahá'u'lláh is the pro-   23
motion of education. Every child must be instructed
in sciences as much as is necessary. If the parents are
able to provide the expenses of this education, it is well,
otherwise the community must provide the means for
the teaching of that child.

And among the teachings of Bahá'u'lláh are justice   24
and right. Until these are realized on the plane of existence, all things shall be in disorder and remain imperfect. The world of mankind is a world of oppression
and cruelty, and a realm of aggression and error.

In fine, such teachings are numerous. These mani-   25
fold principles, which constitute the greatest basis for
the felicity of mankind and are of the bounties of the
Merciful, must be added to the matter of universal
peace and combined with it, so that results may accrue.
Otherwise the realization of universal peace by itself
in the world of mankind is difficult. As the teachings
of Bahá'u'lláh are combined with universal peace, they
are like a table provided with every kind of fresh and
delicious food. Every soul can find, at that table of
infinite bounty, that which he desires. If the question
is restricted to universal peace alone, the remarkable
results which are expected and desired will not be
attained. The scope of universal peace must be such
that all the communities and religions may find their
highest wish realized in it. The teachings of Bahá'u'lláh

are such that all the communities of the world, whether religious, political or ethical, ancient or modern, find in them the expression of their highest wish.

26      For example, the people of religions find, in the teachings of Bahá'u'lláh, the establishment of Universal Religion—a religion that perfectly conforms with present conditions, which in reality effects the immediate cure of the incurable disease, which relieves every pain, and bestows the infallible antidote for every deadly poison. For if we wish to arrange and organize the world of mankind in accordance with the present religious imitations and thereby to establish the felicity of the world of mankind, it is impossible and impracticable— for example, the enforcement of the laws of the Torah and also of the other religions in accordance with present imitations. But the essential basis of all the Divine Religions which pertains to the virtues of the world of mankind and is the foundation of the welfare of the world of man, is found in the teachings of Bahá'u'lláh in the most perfect presentation.

27      Similarly, with regard to the peoples who clamor for freedom: the moderate freedom which guarantees the welfare of the world of mankind and maintains and preserves the universal relationships, is found in its fullest power and extension in the teachings of Bahá'u'lláh.

28      So with regard to political parties: that which is the greatest policy directing the world of mankind, nay,

rather, the Divine policy, is found in the teachings of Bahá'u'lláh.

Likewise with regard to the party of "equality" which   29
seeks the solution of the economic problems: until now
all proposed solutions have proved impracticable except
the economic proposals in the teachings of Bahá'u'lláh
which are practicable and cause no distress to society.

So with the other parties: when ye look deeply into   30
this matter, ye will discover that the highest aims of
those parties are found in the teachings of Bahá'u'lláh.
These teachings constitute the all-inclusive power
among all men and are practicable. But there are some
teachings of the past, such as those of the Torah, which
cannot be carried out at the present day. It is the same
with the other religions and the tenets of the various
sects and the different parties.

For example, the question of universal peace, about   31
which Bahá'u'lláh says that the Supreme Tribunal
must be established: although the League of Nations
has been brought into existence, yet it is incapable of
establishing universal peace. But the Supreme Tribunal
which Bahá'u'lláh has described will fulfil this sacred
task with the utmost might and power. And His plan is
this: that the national assemblies of each country and
nation—that is to say parliaments—should elect two or
three persons who are the choicest of that nation, and
are well informed concerning international laws and the
relations between governments and aware of the essen-

tial needs of the world of humanity in this day. The number of these representatives should be in proportion to the number of inhabitants of that country. The election of these souls who are chosen by the national assembly, that is, the parliament, must be confirmed by the upper house, the congress and the cabinet and also by the president or monarch so these persons may be the elected ones of all the nation and the government. The Supreme Tribunal will be composed of these people, and all mankind will thus have a share therein, for every one of these delegates is fully representative of his nation. When the Supreme Tribunal gives a ruling on any international question, either unanimously or by majority rule, there will no longer be any pretext for the plaintiff or ground of objection for the defendant. In case any of the governments or nations, in the execution of the irrefutable decision of the Supreme Tribunal, be negligent or dilatory, the rest of the nations will rise up against it, because all the governments and nations of the world are the supporters of this Supreme Tribunal. Consider what a firm foundation this is! But by a limited and restricted League the purpose will not be realized as it ought and should. This is the truth about the situation, which has been stated.[2]

32    Consider how powerful are the teachings of Bahá'u'lláh. At a time when He was in the prison of 'Akká and was under the restrictions and threats of two bloodthirsty kings, His teachings, notwithstanding this

fact, spread with all power in Persia and other countries. Should any teaching, or any principle, or any community fall under the threat of a powerful and bloodthirsty monarch, it would be annihilated within a short space of time. At present and for fifty years the Bahá'ís in Persia and most regions have been under severe restrictions and the threat of sword and spear. Thousands of souls have given their lives in the arena of sacrifice and have fallen as victims under the swords of oppression and cruelty. Thousands of esteemed families have been uprooted and destroyed. Thousands of children have been made fatherless. Thousands of fathers have been bereft of their sons. Thousands of mothers have wept and lamented for their boys who have been beheaded. All this oppression and cruelty, rapacity and blood-thirstiness did not hinder or prevent the spread of the teachings of Bahá'u'lláh. They spread more and more every day, and their power and might became more evident.

It may be that some foolish person among the Persians will affix his name to the contents of the Tablets of Bahá'u'lláh or to the explanations given in the letters of 'Abdu'l-Bahá and send it to that esteemed Assembly. Ye must be aware of this fact, for any Persian who seeks fame or has some other intention will take the entire contents of the Tablets of Bahá'u'lláh and publish them in his own name or in that of his community, just as happened at the Universal Races Congress in London

33

before the war. A Persian took the substance of the Epistles of Bahá'u'lláh, entered that Congress, gave them forth in his own name and published them, whereas the wording was exactly that of Bahá'u'lláh. Some such souls have gone to Europe and have caused confusion in the minds of the people of Europe and have disturbed the thoughts of some Orientalists. Ye must bear this fact in mind, for not a word of these teachings was heard in Persia before the appearance of Bahá'u'lláh. Investigate this matter so that it may become to you evident and manifest. Some souls are like parrots. They learn any note which they may hear, and sing it, but they themselves are unaware of what they utter. There is a sect in Persia at present made up of a few souls who are called Bábís, who claim to be followers of the Báb, whereas they are utterly unaware of Him. They have some secret teachings which are entirely opposed to the teachings of Bahá'u'lláh and in Persia people know this. But when these souls come to Europe, they conceal their own teachings and utter those of Bahá'u'lláh, for they know that the teachings of Bahá'u'lláh are powerful and they therefore declare publicly those teachings of Bahá'u'lláh in their own name. As to their secret teachings, they say that they are taken from the Bayán and the Bayán is from the Báb. When ye obtain the translation of the Bayán, which has been translated in Persia, ye will discover the truth that the teachings of Bahá'u'lláh are utterly opposed to the teachings of this sect. Beware lest ye disregard this fact. Should ye desire to investigate the matter further, inquire from Persia.

In brief, when you traverse the regions of the world, 34 thou shalt conclude that all progress is the result of association and cooperation, while ruin is the outcome of animosity and hatred. Notwithstanding this, the world of humanity does not take warning, nor does it awake from the slumber of heedlessness. Man is still causing differences, quarrels and strife in order to marshal the cohorts of war and, with his legions, rush into the field of bloodshed and slaughter.

Then again, consider the phenomenon of compo- 35 sition and decomposition, of existence and non-existence. Every created thing in the contingent world is made up of many and varied atoms, and its existence is dependent on the composition of these. In other words, a conjunction of simple elements takes place so that from this composition a distinct organism is produced. The existence of all things is based upon this principle. But when the order is deranged, decomposition is produced and disintegration sets in, then that thing ceases to exist. That is, the annihilation of all things is caused by decomposition and disintegration. Therefore attraction and composition between the various elements is the means of life, and discord, and division produce death. Thus the cohesive and attractive forces in all things lead to the appearance of fruitful results and effects, while estrangement and alienation of things lead to disturbance and annihilation. Through affinity and attraction all living things like plants, animals and men come into existence, while division and discord bring about decomposition and destruction.

36    Consequently, that which is conducive to association and attraction and unity among the sons of men is the means of the life of the world of humanity, and whatever causes division, repulsion and remoteness leads to the death of humankind.

37    And if, as you pass by fields and plantations, where the plants, flowers and sweet-smelling herbs are growing luxuriantly together, forming a pattern of unity, this is an evidence of the fact that that plantation and garden is flourishing under the care of a skillful gardener. But when you see it in a state of disorder and irregularity you infer that it has lacked the training of an efficient farmer and thus has produced weeds and tares.

38    It therefore becomes manifest that amity and cohesion are indicative of the training of the Real Educator, and dispersion and separation a proof of savagery and deprivation of divine education.

39    A critic may object, saying that peoples, races, tribes and communities of the world are of different and varied customs, habits, tastes, character, inclinations and ideas, that opinions and thoughts are contrary to one another, and how, therefore, is it possible for real unity to be revealed and perfect accord among human souls to exist?

In answer we say that differences are of two kinds. 40
One is the cause of annihilation and is like the antip-
athy existing among warring nations and conflicting
tribes who seek each other's destruction, uprooting one
another's families, depriving one another of rest and
comfort and unleashing carnage, and this is blameworthy. The other kind which is a token of diversity is the
essence of perfection and the cause of the appearance
of divine bestowals.

Consider the flowers of a garden: though differing 41
in kind, color, form and shape, yet, inasmuch as they
are refreshed by the waters of one spring, revived by
the breath of one wind, invigorated by the rays of one
sun, this diversity increases their charm, and adds unto
their beauty. Thus when that unifying force, the penetrating influence of the Word of God, takes effect, the
difference of customs, manners, habits, ideas, opinions
and dispositions embellishes the world of humanity,
and this is praiseworthy. This diversity, this difference
is like the naturally created dissimilarity and variety of
the limbs and organs of the human body, for each one
contributes to the beauty, efficiency and perfection of
the whole. When these different limbs and organs come
under the influence of man's sovereign soul, and the
soul's power pervades the limbs and members, veins
and arteries of the body, then difference reinforces harmony, diversity strengthens love, and multiplicity is the
greatest factor for coordination.

42    How unpleasing to the eye if all the flowers and plants, the leaves and blossoms, the fruits, the branches and the trees of that garden were all of the same shape and color! Diversity of hues, form and shape, enriches and adorns the garden, and heightens the effect thereof. In like manner, when divers shades of thought, temperament and character, are brought together under the power and influence of one central agency, the beauty and glory of human perfection will be revealed and made manifest. Naught but the celestial potency of the Word of God, which rules and transcends the realities of all things, is capable of harmonizing the divergent thoughts, sentiments, ideas, and convictions of the children of men. Verily, it is the penetrating power in all things, the mover of souls and the binder and regulator in the world of humanity.

43    Praise be to God, today the splendor of the Word of God has illumined every horizon, and from all sects, races, tribes, nations, and communities souls have come together in the light of one Word, assembled, united and agreed in perfect harmony.

44    Some time ago, during the war, a letter was written regarding the teachings of Bahá'u'lláh which may appropriately be appended to this epistle.[3]

***

45    O peoples of the world! The Sun of Truth hath risen to illumine the whole earth, and to spiritualize the com-

munity of man. Laudable are the results and the fruits thereof, abundant the holy evidences deriving from this grace. This is mercy unalloyed and purest bounty; it is light for the world and all its peoples; it is harmony and fellowship, and love and solidarity; indeed it is compassion and unity, and the end of foreignness; it is the being at one, in complete dignity and freedom, with all on earth.

The Blessed Beauty saith: "Ye are all the fruits of one  46 tree, the leaves of one branch." Thus hath He likened this world of being to a single tree, and all its peoples to the leaves thereof, and the blossoms and fruits. It is needful for the bough to blossom, and leaf and fruit to flourish, and upon the interconnection of all parts of the world-tree, dependeth the flourishing of leaf and blossom, and the sweetness of the fruit.

For this reason must all human beings powerfully  47 sustain one another and seek for everlasting life; and for this reason must the lovers of God in this contingent world become the mercies and the blessings sent forth by that clement King of the seen and unseen realms. Let them purify their sight and behold all humankind as leaves and blossoms and fruits of the tree of being. Let them at all times concern themselves with doing a kindly thing for one of their fellows, offering to someone love, consideration, thoughtful help. Let them see no one as their enemy, or as wishing them ill, but think of all humankind as their friends; regarding the alien as an intimate, the stranger as a companion, staying free of prejudice, drawing no lines.

48    In this day, the one favored at the Threshold of the Lord is he who handeth round the cup of faithfulness; who bestoweth, even upon his enemies, the jewel of bounty, and lendeth, even to his fallen oppressor, a helping hand; it is he who will, even to the fiercest of his foes, be a loving friend. These are the Teachings of the Blessed Beauty, these the counsels of the Most Great Name.

49    O ye dear friends! The world is at war and the human race is in travail and mortal combat. The dark night of hate hath taken over, and the light of good faith is blotted out. The peoples and kindreds of the earth have sharpened their claws, and are hurling themselves one against the other. It is the very foundation of the human race that is being destroyed. It is thousands of households that are vagrant and dispossessed, and every year seeth thousands upon thousands of human beings weltering in their lifeblood on dusty battlefields. The tents of life and joy are down. The generals practice their generalship, boasting of the blood they shed, competing one with the next in inciting to violence. "With this sword," saith one of them, "I beheaded a people!" And another: "I toppled a nation to the ground!" And yet another: "I brought a government down!" On such things do men pride themselves, in such do they glory!

Love—righteousness—these are everywhere censured, while despised are harmony, and devotion to the truth.

The Faith of the Blessed Beauty is summoning mankind to safety and love, to amity and peace; it hath raised up its tabernacle on the heights of the earth, and directeth its call to all nations. Wherefore, O ye who are God's lovers, know ye the value of this precious Faith, obey its teachings, walk in this road that is drawn straight, and show ye this way to the people. Lift up your voices and sing out the song of the Kingdom. Spread far and wide the precepts and counsels of the loving Lord, so that this world will change into another world, and this darksome earth will be flooded with light, and the dead body of mankind will arise and live; so that every soul will ask for immortality, through the holy breaths of God. 50

Soon will your swiftly passing days be over, and the fame and riches, the comforts, the joys provided by this rubbish-heap, the world, will be gone without a trace. Summon ye, then, the people to God, and invite humanity to follow the example of the Company on high. Be ye loving fathers to the orphan, and a refuge to the helpless, and a treasury for the poor, and a cure for the ailing. Be ye the helpers of every victim of oppression, the patrons of the disadvantaged. Think ye at all times of rendering some service to every member of the human race. Pay ye no heed to aversion and rejection, to 51 disdain, hostility, injustice: act ye in the opposite way. Be ye sincerely kind, not in appearance only. Let each one of God's loved ones center his attention on this: to be the Lord's mercy to man; to be the Lord's grace. Let him do some good to every person whose path he crosseth, and be of some benefit to him. Let him improve the character of each and all, and reorient the minds of men. In this way, the light of divine guidance will shine forth, and the blessings of God will cradle all mankind: for love is light, no matter in what abode it dwelleth; and hate is darkness, no matter where it may make its nest. O friends of God! That the hidden Mystery may stand revealed, and the secret essence of all things may be disclosed, strive ye to banish that darkness for ever and ever.

# 2

## Second Tablet to The Hague
## 1 July 1920

To the esteemed members of the Executive Committee of the Central Organization for a Durable Peace

Your reply, dated 12 June 1920, to my letter was received with the utmost gratitude. God be praised, it testified to the unity of thought and purpose that existeth between us and you, and expressed sentiments of the heart that bear the hallmark of sincere affection.  1

We Bahá'ís have the greatest affinity for your esteemed organization, and dispatched therefore two distinguished individuals to you in order to forge a strong bond. For in this day the cause of universal peace is of paramount importance amongst all human affairs and is the greatest instrument for securing the very life and felicity of mankind. Bereft of this effulgent reality, humanity can  2 in no wise find true composure or real advancement but will, day by day, sink ever deeper into misery and wretchedness.

3    This last terrible war hath clearly proven that humanity cannot withstand the effects of modern instruments of warfare. The future can in no wise be compared to the past, for earlier weapons and armaments had but a feeble effect, whilst modern ones can, in a brief span of time, strike at the very roots of the world of humanity and surpass the limits of its endurance.

4    In this age, therefore, universal peace is like unto the sun, which bestoweth life upon all things, and it is thus incumbent upon all to endeavor in the path of this mighty cause. Now, we indeed share this common goal with you and strive toward it with all our strength, renouncing even our lives, our kindred, and our substance for its sake.

5    As ye have no doubt heard, in Persia thousands of souls have offered up their lives in this path, and thousands of homes have been laid waste. Despite this, we have in no wise relented, but have continued to endeavor unto this very moment and are increasing our efforts as day followeth day, because our desire for peace is not derived merely from the intellect: It is a matter of religious belief and one of the eternal foundations of the Faith of God. That is why we strive with all our might and, forsaking our own advantage, rest, and comfort, forgo the pursuit of our own affairs; devote ourselves

to the mighty cause of peace; and consider it to be the very foundation of the Divine religions, a service to His Kingdom, the source of eternal life, and the greatest means of admittance into the heavenly realm.

Today the benefits of universal peace are recognized 6 amongst the people, and likewise the harmful effects of war are clear and manifest to all. But in this matter, knowledge alone is far from sufficient: A power of implementation is needed to establish it throughout the world. Ye should therefore consider how the compelling power of conscience can be awakened, so that this lofty ideal may be translated from the realm of thought into that of reality. For it is clear and evident that the execution of this mighty endeavor is impossible through ordinary human feelings but requireth the powerful sentiments of the heart to transform its potential into reality.

Indeed, all on earth know that an upright character 7 is praiseworthy and acceptable and that baseness of character is blameworthy and rejected, that justice and fairness are favored and agreeable whilst cruelty and tyranny are unacceptable and rejected. Notwithstanding this, all people, but for a few, are devoid of a praiseworthy character and bereft of a sense of justice.

The power of conscience is therefore needed, and 8 spiritual sentiments are required, that souls may feel compelled to evince a goodly character. It is our firm belief that the power of implementation in this great endeavor is the penetrating influence of the Word of God and the confirmations of the Holy Spirit.

9    We are bound to you by the strongest ties of love and unity. We long with heart and soul for the day to arrive when the tabernacle of the oneness of humanity will have been raised in the midmost heart of the world and the banner of universal peace unfurled in all regions. The oneness of humanity must therefore be established, that the edifice of universal peace may be raised in turn.

10    Your organization, which is a well-wisher of the world of humanity, is highly esteemed in the eyes of the Bahá'ís. Therefore kindly accept our highest regards and keep us ever informed of the progress of the cause of universal peace in Europe through your efforts. We hope that our communications will remain constant.

# Additional Tablets

# 3

*He is God!*

O thou dear handmaid of God!　1

Thy letter dated 6 April 1906 hath been　2
received. Thou hast written that . . . hath regained her
health. God be praised, this daughter of the Kingdom
hath attained unto spiritual health. A disaster to the
body, when spiritual health is present, is of no importance. That is the main thing. God be thanked, she
hath attained that great bestowal; she hath taken on
immortal life.

It is to be regretted, however, that her husband is still　3
wrapped in the veils of his idle imaginings. If her dear
daughter . . . be trained according to the instructions of
God, she will grow to be a peerless plant in the garden

of the heart. It is incumbent upon the father to choose for his daughter the glory that dieth not. Nevertheless, this is up to him; he may educate her in any way he desireth.

4 As to what thou didst ask regarding the history of the philosophers: history, prior to Alexander of Greece, is extremely confused, for it is a fact that only after Alexander did history become an orderly and systematized discipline. One cannot, for this reason, rely upon traditions and reported historical events that have come down from before the days of Alexander. This is a matter thoroughly established, in the view of all authoritative historians. How many a historical account was taken as fact in the eighteenth century, yet the opposite was proved true in the nineteenth. No reliance, then, can be placed upon the traditions and reports of historians which antedate Alexander, not even with regard to ascertaining the lifetimes of leading individuals.

5 Wherefore ye should not be surprised that the Tablet of Wisdom is in conflict with the historical accounts. It behooveth one to reflect a while on the great diversity of opinion among the historians, and their contradictory accounts; for the historians of East and West are much at odds, and the Tablet of Wisdom was written in accordance with certain histories of the East.

6 Furthermore, the Torah, held to be the most ancient of histories, existeth today in three separate versions: the Hebrew, considered authentic by the Jews and the

Protestant clergy; the Greek Septuagint, which is used as authoritative in the Greek and other Eastern churches; and the Samaritan Torah, the standard authority for that people. These three versions differ greatly, one from another, even with regard to the lifetimes of the most celebrated figures.

In the Hebrew Torah, it is recorded that from Noah's 7 flood until the birth of Abraham there was an interval of two hundred and ninety-two years. In the Greek, that time-span is given as one thousand and seventy-two years, while in the Samaritan, the recorded span is nine hundred and forty-two years. Refer to the commentary by Henry Westcott,[4] for tables are supplied therein which show the discrepancies among the three Torahs as to the birthdates of a number of the descendants of Shem, and thou wilt see how greatly the versions differ one from another.

Moreover, according to the text of the Hebrew 8 Torah, from the creation of Adam until Noah's flood the elapsed time is recorded as one thousand six hundred and fifty-six years, while in the Greek Torah the interval is given as two thousand two hundred and sixty-two years, and in the Samaritan text, the same period is said to have lasted one thousand three hundred and seven years.

Reflect thou now over the discrepancies among these 9 three Torahs. The case is indeed surprising. The Jews and Protestants belittle the Greek Torah, while to the

Greeks, the Hebrew version is spurious, and the Samaritans deny both the Hebrew and the Greek versions.

10 Our purpose is to show that even in Scriptural history, the most outstanding of all histories, there are contradictions as to the time when the great ones lived, let alone as to dates related to others. And furthermore, learned societies in Europe are continually revising the existing records, both of East and West. In spite of this, how can the confused accounts of peoples dating from before Alexander be compared with the Holy Text of God? If any scholar expresses astonishment, let him be surprised at the discrepancies in Scriptural history.

11 Nevertheless, Holy Writ is authoritative, and with it no history of the world can compare, for experience hath shown that after investigation of the facts and a thorough study of ancient records and corroborative evidence, all have referred back to the Holy Scriptures. The most important thing is to establish the validity of God's universal Manifestation; once His claim proveth true, then whatsoever He may choose to say is right and correct.

12 The histories prior to Alexander, which were based on oral accounts current among the people, were put together later on. There are great discrepancies among them, and certainly they can never hold their own against Holy Writ. It is an accepted fact among historians themselves that these histories were compiled after Alexander, and that prior to his time history was

transmitted by word of mouth. Note how extremely confused was the history of Greece, so much so that to this day there is no agreement on the dates related to the life of Homer, Greece's far-famed poet. Some even maintain that Homer never existed at all, and that the name is a fabrication.

A letter hath been addressed to Mr. Sprague, thou wilt find it enclosed. 13

It is my hope that through the favor and grace of the Abhá Beauty, thou wilt fully recover thy health, and engage in serving the Cause with all thy might. I am aware that thou art much afflicted, and in extreme distress; but if we taste a drop from affliction's cup, the Blessed Beauty drank down a sea of anguish, and once we call this to mind, then every hardship turneth into peaceful rest, and toil into merciful bliss. Then will a draught of agony be but refreshing wine, and the tyrant's wound only a friend's most gentle balm. Greetings be unto thee, and praise. 14

# 4

Paris
The Friends of God,
Upon them rest the glory of God, the All-Glorious!

*He is God!*

1 O loved ones of 'Abdu'l-Bahá!

2 Praise be to God! The fragrances of holiness are spread abroad. The pearls of bounty are scattered everywhere. The light of guidance is resplendent. The morning-star of the Concourse on High ascendeth. The cloud of mercy raineth down. The sun of bestowal blazeth and dazzleth. The wind of providence bloweth, and the fragrances of the Abhá Paradise nourish souls in the North and South. The East is illumined, and the West scented with roses. The world is perfumed with musk. Blessed is he who hath illumined his eyes by

beholding these splendors and whose soul hath become a garden through inhaling this musk-scented breeze.

O loved ones of God! Now is the time to be drunk 3 with the cup of the Covenant. Rend your garments in love for the beauty of the All-Merciful. In the banquet of the Covenant seize ye the chalice of divine knowledge. Drunk and yearning, raise up a song of the purity and sanctity of the Living, the Almighty God, till East and West are bewitched, and North and South set ablaze.

# 5

1    O flame of the love of God! The ray must shed light and the sun must rise; the full moon must shine and the star must gleam. Since thou art a ray, beseech thou the Lord to enable thee to give illumination and enlightenment, to brighten the horizons and to consume the world with the fire of the love of God. I hope that thou mayest attain such a station, nay, surpass it. Upon thee be His glory.

# 6

O ye sons and daughters of the Kingdom!    1

Your letter dated September 30 of this year    2
hath been received, and from the contents it became
clear and evident that the fire of the love of God hath
burst into a flame in that region—a flame that can illumine the whole world and transform the East and the
West into a field for the knights of the Kingdom.

Consider how all the peoples of the world are slum-    3
bering upon the couch of negligence, but praise be to
God, ye have been awakened. All men remain sunk in
heedlessness, but ye have become quick of apprehen-
sion. They are deprived of the blessings of the Kingdom, but ye are among the well-favored. Neither the
crow nor the raven can take part in the delights of a
sparkling rose-garden; the charm and perfection of the
rose are as nourishment to the impassioned nightingale
endowed with a melodious voice. The realm of the

Kingdom is like the fountain of life and ye are as the fish, sore athirst and restless.

4    Render ye thanks unto God, inasmuch as in the Day of the advent of the Kingdom ye have drawn so nigh unto His court and are so greatly favored at the Threshold of the loving Lord. Therefore it behooveth you to strive with heart and soul so that the human world may shine resplendent, that the basis of hatred and antagonism may be wiped out from the earth and that all mankind may live together in unity and harmony, with the utmost love and fellowship.

# 7

Praise be to God that ye are present in this radiant 1
assemblage and have turned your faces toward the
Kingdom of Abhá! That which ye behold is from the
grace and bounty of the Blessed Perfection. We are
as atoms and He is the Sun of Truth. We are as drops
and He is the Most Great Ocean. Poor are we, yet the
outpouring of the treasury of the Kingdom is boundless. Weak are we, yet the confirmation of the Supreme
Concourse is abundant. Helpless are we, yet our refuge
and shelter is Bahá'u'lláh.

Praise be to God! His signs are evident. 2

Praise be to God! His light is shining. 3

Praise be to God! His ocean is surging. 4

Praise be to God! His radiance is intense. 5

Praise be to God! His bestowals are abundant. 6

Praise be to God! His favors are manifest. 7

Glad tidings! Glad tidings! The Morn of Guidance 8
hath dawned.

9      Glad tidings! Glad tidings! The Sun of Truth hath shone forth.

10      Glad tidings! Glad tidings! The breeze of favor hath wafted.

11      Glad tidings! Glad tidings! The showers of the clouds of divine bounty have poured down.

12      Glad tidings! Glad tidings! The Sun of the supreme horizon hath shed its radiance upon all the world with boundless effulgence.

13      Glad tidings! Glad tidings! The hearts of all are in the utmost purity.

14      Glad tidings! Glad tidings! His all-encompassing splendor hath been revealed.

15      Glad tidings! Glad tidings! The celestial concourse is astir.

16      Glad tidings! Glad tidings! Zion is rapt in ecstasy.

17      Glad tidings! Glad tidings! The Kingdom of God is filled with exultation and joy.[5]

# 8

O ye two pilgrims of the Holy Shrine! 1
The news of your safe arrival in Paris was 2
received and rejoiced my heart, as did the description of
the love and devotion of the friends in Paris, who met
you with exceeding joy and radiance, and who show
forth the utmost love, faithfulness, and sincerity.

Speak openly of all the signs of the Kingdom of God 3
that ye have witnessed with your own eyes and share
with the utmost happiness and exultation all that ye
have heard of the divine teachings. I fervently suppli-
cate God to bring assurance to your souls and to raise
you up with such steadfastness that each of you may
withstand an entire nation. May you become so inebri-
ated with the wine of the love of God that ye may cause
your hearers to dance with blissful rapture to the song
and melody of the love of God.

This is the time for gladness, the day of joy and 4
exhilaration, for, praised be God, all doors are opened

wide through the bounty of the Abhá Beauty. But high endeavor and self-sacrifice are needed and the concentration of one's thoughts is required for the tree of hope to yield its fruit and results to be achieved.

# 9

O ye two honorable souls! 1

Your letter was received and its contents 2
noted. My heart was saddened to learn that those two
respected persons, who were even as one soul, should
now be separated and their affection turned into
estrangement.

Although divorce is permissible, yet it is strongly 3
abhorred and condemned in the sight of God. Divorce
may only take place when no alternative is left, when
the two parties feel aversion for each other and are in
torment. Now, if such is the case, perform the divorce.
However, after divorce is decided upon, ye must wait
for one year for it to be effected. Should affection be
renewed during this year of separation, it would be
highly pleasing.

The Glory of Glories rest upon you both! 4

5    If divorce taketh place, the spiritual love and affection between you should increase, and ye should become like a brother and sister.

# Extracts from Tablets

# 10

I n this day, no greater manifestation of love and kind- 1 ness can be conceived in the world of existence than this, that, at the Shrine of Bahá'u'lláh, one should call to mind a loved one, make mention of him, and offer prayers for his well-being. This is God's mightiest favor, His greatest bounty, His highest gift, and the sign of His consummate bestowal.

# 11

1 Convey warmest, most loving greetings to Mark Tobey on my behalf, and heartfelt affection to Marguerite Bull.[6] What a sacred task is hers, serving helpless children! I ask God to assist her.

2 As for thee, obey the Convention,[7] travel for a time, and teach. After that, work to perfect thine art. For it is incumbent upon thee both to obey the Convention, and to perfect thine art.

3 I rejoice to hear that thou takest pains with thine art, for in this wonderful new age, art is worship. The more thou strivest to perfect it, the closer wilt thou come to God. What bestowal could be greater than this, that one's art should be even as the act of worshipping the Lord? That is to say, when thy fingers grasp the paint-brush, it is as if thou wert at prayer in the Temple.

# 12

Shouldst thou recite any of the revealed prayers, 1
and seek assistance from God with thy face turned
towards Him, and implore Him with devotion and fervor, thy need will be answered.

# 13

1 Know thou that before maturity man liveth from day to day and comprehendeth only such matters as are superficial and outwardly obvious. However, when he cometh of age he understandeth the realities of things and the inner truths. Indeed, in his comprehension, his feelings, his deductions and his discoveries, every day of his life after maturity is equal to a year before it.

# 14

Know ye that the Torah is what was revealed in the 1
Tablets unto Moses, may peace be upon Him,
and in that which He was commanded to do. But the
stories are historical narratives and were written after
Moses, may peace be upon Him. . . . The glorious
Book, the Mighty Decree, is what was in the Tablets
which Moses, upon Him be peace, brought from Mt.
Sinai, and that which He proclaimed unto the Children
of Israel, in accordance with the explicit text of those
Tablets.

# 15

1 It is the wish of my heart and soul that the Sun of the divine heavens will shine with such splendor and beauty in that country that India will become a rose-garden. . . . India will sweeten the palates with delectable sweetness, will mingle ambergris and musk, and mix milk with honey.

# 16

It may be that letters addressed to the women believ- 1 ers do indeed contain certain passages written by way of encouragement, but the purpose of such passages is to show that, in this wondrous Dispensation, certain women have outshone certain men—not that all women have excelled all men! The members of the Spiritual Assembly should do all they can to give encouragement to the women. In this Dispensation one should not think in terms of "men" and "women": all are under the shadow of the Word of God and, as they strive more diligently, so shall their reward be greater— be they men or women or the frailest of people. . . . As for the large number of Tablets addressed to women enjoining them to teach the Cause: since the letters arriving in the Holy Land come for the most part from women, and only rarely from men, it is natural that women should be written to more frequently than men.

. . .

2    As to thy question: "To whom should we turn?"—turn thou to the Ancient Beauty. God willing, a copy of His blessed portrait will in due course be dispatched to thee so that when offering prayer thou mayest turn thyself in spirit towards that Holy Likeness, and not towards some mere figment of the imagination. Know thou, however, that at no time should His blessed portrait be hung in the Mashriqu'l-Adhkár.

3    As regards the question of young children and of weak, defenseless souls who are afflicted at the hands of the oppressor, in this a great wisdom is concealed. The question is one of cardinal importance, but briefly it may be stated that in the world to come a mighty recompense awaiteth such souls. Much, indeed, might be said upon this theme, and upon how the afflictions that they bear in life become a cause for them of such an outpouring of Divine mercy and bestowal as is preferable to a hundred thousand earthly comforts and to a world of growth and development in this transitory abode; but, if possible, God willing, all this will be explained to thee in detail and by word of mouth when thou arrivest here.

# 17

Know thou that the distinction between male and  1
female is an exigency of the physical world and
hath no connection with the spirit; for the spirit and the
world of the spirit are sanctified above such exigencies,
and wholly beyond the reach of such changes as befall
the physical body in the contingent world. In former
ages, men enjoyed ascendancy over women because
bodily might reigned supreme and the spirit was subject
to its dominion. In this radiant age, however, since the
power of the spirit hath transcended that of the body
and assumed its ascendancy, authority and dominion
over the human world, this physical distinction hath
ceased to be of consequence; and, as the sway and influence of the spirit have become apparent, women have
come to be the full equals of men. Today, therefore,
there is no respect or circumstance in which a person's
sex provideth grounds for the exercise of either discrim-
ination or favor.

# 18

1   In ancient times the people of America were, through their northern regions, close to Asia, that is, separated from Asia by a strait. For this reason, it hath been said that crossing had occurred. There are other signs which indicate communication.

2   As to places whose people were not informed of the appearance of Prophets, such people are excused. In the Qur'án it hath been revealed: "We will not chastise them if they had not been sent a Messenger."[8]

3   Undoubtedly in those regions the Call of God must have been raised in ancient times, but it hath been forgotten now.

# 19

The Bayán hath been superseded by the Kitáb-i-Aqdas, except in respect of such laws as have been confirmed and mentioned in the Kitáb-i-Aqdas. The Book to which the Bahá'ís turn is the Kitáb-i-Aqdas, not the Bayán.

# 20

1   I eagerly anticipate the day when New York will become a blessed spot from which the call to steadfastness in the Covenant of God will go forth to every part of the world, thus making that city outstanding from every point of view.

2   Bless Thou, O King of Kings, the city of New York! Cause the friends there to be kind to one another. Purify their souls and make their hearts to be free and detached. Illumine the world of their consciousness. Exhilarate their spirits and bestow celestial power and confirmation upon them. Establish there a heavenly realm, so that the City of Bahá may prosper and New York be favored with blessings from the Abhá Kingdom, that this region may become like the all-highest Paradise, may develop into a vineyard of God and be transformed into a heavenly orchard and a spiritual rose-garden.

# 21

The question of economics must commence with    1
the farmer and then be extended to the other
classes inasmuch as the number of farmers is far greater
than all other classes. Therefore, it is fitting to begin
with the farmer in matters related to economics for
the farmer is the first active agent in human society. In
brief, from among the wise men in every village a board
should be set up and the affairs of that village should
be under the control of that board. Likewise a general
storehouse should be founded with the appointment of
a secretary. At the time of the harvest, under the direction of that board, a certain percentage of the entire
harvest should be appropriated for the storehouse.

The storehouse has seven revenues: Tithes, taxes on    2
animals, property without an heir, all lost objects found
whose owners cannot be traced, one third of all treasure-
trove, one third of the produce of all mines, and voluntary contributions.

3      This storehouse also has seven expenditures:

1. General running expenses of the storehouse, such as the salary of the secretary and the administration of public health.
2. Tithes to the government.
3. Taxes on animals to the government.
4. Costs of running an orphanage.
5. Costs of running a home for the incapacitated.
6. Costs of running a school.
7. Payment of subsidies to provide needed support of the poor.

4      The first revenue is the tithe. It should be collected as follows: If, for instance, the income of a person is five hundred dollars and his necessary expenses are the same, no tithes will be collected from him. If another's expenses are five hundred dollars while his income is one thousand dollars, one tenth will be taken from him, for he hath more than his needs; if he giveth one tenth of the surplus, his livelihood will not be adversely affected. If another's expenses are one thousand dollars, and his income is five thousand dollars, as he hath four thousand dollars surplus he will be required to give one and a half tenths. If another person hath necessary expenses of one thousand dollars, but his income is ten thousand dollars, from him two tenths will be required for his surplus represents a large sum. But if

the necessary expenses of another person are four or five thousand dollars, and his income one hundred thousand, one fourth will be required from him. On the other hand, should a person's income be two hundred, but his needs absolutely essential for his livelihood be five hundred dollars, and provided he hath not been remiss in his work or his farm hath not been blessed with a harvest, such a one must receive help from the general storehouse so that he may not remain in need and may live in comfort.

A certain amount must be put aside from the general 5 storehouse for the orphans of the village and a certain sum for the incapacitated. A certain amount must be provided from this storehouse for those who are needy and incapable of earning a livelihood, and a certain amount for the village's system of education. And, a certain amount must be set aside for the administration of public health. If anything is left in the storehouse, that must be transferred to the general treasury of the nation for national expenditures.

# 22

1   O ye beloved friends of God and handmaids of the Merciful!

2   Call ye to mind the blessed Name of our peerless Beloved, the Abhá Beauty, in an uplifting spirit of unbounded ecstasy and delight, then unloose your tongues in His praise in such wise that the realm of the heart may be purged from the woes and sorrows of the world of water and clay, that the great heights of spiritual perception may be unveiled before your eyes, that the glorious signs of His Divine Unity may shine resplendent, a fresh outpouring of His grace may stream forth, and a liberal effusion of celestial confirmations may be vouchsafed unto you.

3   His Name is indeed the healing medicine for every illness, and imparteth warmth unto those chilled with cold. It is the sovereign remedy and the supreme talisman. It is the source of life in both worlds, and of salvation unto such as have gone astray. Today this hallowed

Name serveth as a shield for all mankind, and as a veritable refuge for the children of men. It is the wondrous accent of the Lord of Mercy, and His celestial melody.

Wherefore, O faithful friends, raise ye the triumphal cry of Yá Bahá'u'l-Abhá! O ye who yearn after the Beauty of the Almighty! Lift up your faces toward the Supreme Horizon. Rest not, even for a moment. Breathe not a single breath save in remembrance of His love and in recognition of His grace, in the promulgation of His Utterances and the vindication of His Testimonies. 4

Verily, this is the Magnet of divine confirmations. This is the mighty Force which will surely attract heavenly assistance. 5

# 23

1    The Ancient Beauty[9]—may my life be offered up for His loved ones—did not to outward seeming meet His Holiness, the Exalted One[10]—may my life be a sacrifice unto Him.

# 24

As for thy question concerning those righteous souls 1
who passed away ere they heard the Call of this
Revelation, know thou that those who ascended unto
God ere they heard this Call, but who followed the precepts of Christ and walked in the Straight Path—these
verily attained, after ascending to the Divine Kingdom,
unto the Refulgent Light.

# 25

1   The residence is under all conditions the property of the first-born son, irrespective of whether or not the deceased should have left behind him other property as well. The first-born son receiveth, moreover, his share of the remainder of the estate. This is that which God hath prescribed. The testator is, however, at liberty while still alive to dispose of his property in whatsoever manner he seeth fit. Likewise, the first-born son must himself, for the sake of God, take into consideration the other heirs, and be just and fair to them. In truth, it is obligatory for everyone, by the express requirement of the divine text, to draw up a will, so that it may be implemented after he hath passed away. This, verily, is the perspicuous truth. If, God forbid, he disobeyeth the divine command—faileth, that is, to draw up a will— then his estate must be divided up in the stipulated manner.

# 26

As for the story of Adam, the Father of Mankind, which is recorded in the Sacred Scriptures, this requireth explanation and interpretation. By "genesis" is intended a spiritual creation and heavenly existence; for otherwise the most cursory reflection would be sufficient to convince even a child that this boundless universe, the world of being—this infinite cosmos, this prodigious system, this mighty and primordial workshop—is far more than six thousand years old, as hath in fact been realized in this illumined age by scientists and men of learning, on the basis of decisive proofs and evidences founded on both reason and discovery. In recent times remains have come to light which have been definitely and conclusively established to be more than ten thousand years old. Through the science of geology this hidden secret hath been grasped—that the age of the world surpasseth man's conception. The one true God hath ever been the Possessor of all Names and

Attributes, and the necessary concomitants of these Names and Attributes have likewise ever existed and shall continue to exist throughout eternity. He Who is the "Creator" requireth a creation, while He Who is the "Provider" requireth some object to provide for. A king, to be a king, must have a realm, an army, the insignia of sovereignty, the retinue and entourage of kingship. The sovereignty of God is everlasting; from time immemorial it hath existed, and at no time hath it been suspended. For a king bereft of troops and territory is a person of no consequence; and were One Who is the 'All-Possessing' to be entirely destitute, know then that no richer harvest would be reaped from His existence than from a fruitless cypress tree.

# 27

O pilgrim of the Sacred Dust!                                    1
    Render a myriad thanks unto the All-Glorious,    2
Who hath guided thee on this path and enabled thee to
attain the threshold of the Omniscient Lord, to find refuge within the stronghold of His favors, and to obtain
that which is the ultimate hope and desire of all His
chosen ones.

Now, as thou returnest to Ishqábád, thou must take    3
with thee armfuls of flowers as a gift from the heavenly rose-garden that their sweet scent may perfume
the nostrils and stir the senses of the youth. For these
lovely youth are the children of the realms above and
the tender plants of the all-highest Paradise. They are
flowers and fragrant herbs in the garden of certitude,
the jasmine and eglantine of the All-Merciful Lord.
They have been nursed at the breast of Divine unity
and nurtured in the bosom of the wondrous Cause of

God. They have become fresh and verdant through the outpourings of the clouds of loving-kindness.

4      O youth of this century of God! In this new age, this century of the Glorious Lord, ye must be so attracted to the Blessed Beauty and so enthralled by the Beloved of the World that ye may become the embodiments of the truth of this verse:

> I am lost, O Love, possessed and dazed,
> Love's fool am I, in all the earth.[11]

# 28

Concerning the question of marriage and the stipu-    1
lated period between the time of the engagement
and the marriage, this is the decisive text of the Book
of God and may not be interpreted. In the past, serious
difficulties and problems arose when a long period of
time elapsed between the engagement and the marriage.
Now, according to the text of the Book, when marriage
between the parties is arranged, i.e., when the parties
become engaged, and it is certain that they will be
married, not more than ninety-five days should elapse
before the marriage takes place, during which period
preparations for the dowry and other affairs may be
made. The marriage ceremony must take place on the
same night as its consummation, that is, there should
be no interval of time between the ceremony and consummation. This is a clear text and is not subject to
interpretation, so that the difficulties that arose in the
past may not recur on account of interpretation.

3

---

# Twelve Table Talks Given by 'Abdu'l-Bahá in 'Akká

# 1

## The Three Kinds of Prophets

Question: How many kinds of divine Prophets are 1 there?

Answer: There are three kinds of divine Prophets. 2 One kind are the universal Manifestations, which are even as the sun. Through Their advent the world of existence is renewed, a new cycle is inaugurated, a new religion is revealed, souls are quickened to a new life, and East and West are flooded with light. These Souls are the universal Manifestations of God and have been sent forth to the entire world and the generality of mankind.

Another kind of Prophets are followers and promul- 3 gators, not leaders and law-givers, but they are nonetheless the recipients of the hidden inspirations of God. Yet another kind are Prophets Whose prophethood has been limited to a particular locality. But the universal

Manifestations are all-encompassing: They are like the root, and all others are as the branches; they are like the sun, and all others are as the moon and the stars.

# 2

## Two Kinds of Prophecy

Question: In the books of the Prophets there are    1
tidings of the future; that is, certain events and
incidents have been explicitly or implicitly announced
and unseen matters foretold, which in this day are witnessed to have come true in their entirety. How were
these events of the present day foreseen in the past?

Answer: The Prophets of God draw upon both His    2
boundless universal grace and His particular grace, that
is, upon divine revelation and inspiration. They foretell
certain events through revelation and inspiration, which
are the heavenly splendors, the intimations of the heart,
and the scattering rays of the light of the Day-Star of
Truth. This grace is like the resplendent rays of the sun,
and the hearts of the Prophets are even as mirrors. Thus
They affirm that Their words have proceeded from revelation and inspiration.

3    The second kind of discovery is due to the fact that the Prophets are able Physicians and informed of the mysteries of the universe. They have Their finger on the pulse of the world, and They diagnose and foresee the ailments and illnesses which are to come. It is from the appearance, signs, and conditions of the universe itself that They infer these mysteries. Thus, when an able physician notes certain signs and symptoms in the body of a patient, he diagnoses future ailments, illnesses, and conditions. This proceeds from his knowledge, skill, and power of inference.

4    But the tidings of the Prophets are all founded upon the scattering rays of the light of truth and proceed from pure inspiration and revelation. For past, present, and future apply only to the world of creation, not to the world of God. In the realm of Truth, past, present, and future are one and the same: The beginning is even as the end and the end even as the beginning. For in the eternal and everlasting realm of God, time holds no sway and no distinction can be made between past and future, as past and future are contrary to that which has neither beginning nor end. In a realm that has no beginning and no end, how can past, present, and future even be imagined? Observe that even in an outward sense time has no sway in the world of the intellect, even though it holds sway in the mind of an intelligent person, for the power of the mind has ever apprehended

and encompassed all things and will forever continue to do so.

Consider for example the sun itself: It knows neither 5 morning, nor noon, nor evening—all times are one; all moments are the same. But on account of the rising and setting of the sun, the inhabitants of the earth see mornings and evenings and reckon the days and nights. Thus all these times are one in the sun and all these days are identical and indistinguishable.

Likewise, in the realm of truth, past, present, and 6 future are the same, and future events are even as past and present occurrences. From the perspective of that realm, all events and incidents take place in the present and are witnessed by the Prophets and the chosen ones. And so it is that the Prophets herald events that will transpire two or three thousand years hence, for they abide in the realm of truth, wherein the mysteries of the universe are revealed and laid bare. Infer from this statement the truth of the spiritual discoveries of the Holy Ones and reflect and ponder thereon—the matter is indeed clear and manifest.

# 3

## The Meaning of Speaking in Tongues[12]

1    Question: What is meant by the Apostles' speaking in tongues?

2    Answer: The meaning is that the Apostles taught in a spiritual tongue, a tongue that embraces all tongues. For the Word of the Kingdom comprises spiritual meanings and divine mysteries, and whoso attains to this Word will find the realities and mysteries of creation to be clear and evident. The divine inner meanings are the all-encompassing reality of all tongues.

3    Therefore, the Holy Spirit endowed the Apostles with the tongue of the Kingdom, and they spoke with all peoples as if in their own tongue; that is, whenever they conversed with a person of any faith or nation, it was as though they were speaking his own tongue. Were it otherwise, there are at present more than a thousand known languages and it would be fair to expect that

the Apostles would have written at least one Gospel in the language of one of the other nations. It is, however, well established that the Gospel was written only in Hebrew and in Greek. No Gospel was even written in Latin, though that was at the time the official language of the land. Yet, as the Apostles were not proficient in Latin, no Gospel was written in that language.

# 4

## The Invocation "He Is God"[13]

1   Question: Why is the expression "He is God" used at the beginning of the Tablets and Epistles?

2   Answer: This is a common practice in the East among the Muslims, and their intent is that one must begin all things with the mention of God. But what is intended in the divine Tablets is that the reality of the divine Essence is sanctified above all understanding, exalted beyond all imagination. For whatsoever man may imagine is encompassed by him, and that which encompasses is without a doubt greater than that which is encompassed. It is therefore clear that what is imagined is the creation, not the Creator. For the reality of Divinity is sanctified above all human fancy. In this day all people are worshippers of idle fancies, for they conceive a god in the realm of imagination and worship him. Thus if you were to ask someone who is

engaged in prayer: "Whom are you worshipping?" he would say: "God." "What God?" "God as I imagine Him." Whereas that which is in his imagination is not God. All people are therefore worshippers of their own thoughts and fancies.

Thus for man there is no path to tread and no place to turn save unto the holy Manifestations. For, as already mentioned, the reality of Divinity is transcendent, sanctified, and beyond all imagination. All that can be imagined are the holy and divine Manifestations. There is nowhere else for man to direct his gaze, and should he pass beyond this he will fall prey to delusion. Thus what is meant by the words "He is God" is that that manifest Being is the promised Beauty and the Day-Star of Truth, the Exponent of the secrets of Lordship and Divinity, the Repository of the mysteries of the All-Merciful, and the Source of the signs of His Singleness; and that I have begun my discourse with His blessed Name.

# 5

## The Wisdom of Fasting[14]

1 Question: What is the divine wisdom of fasting?

2 Answer: There is many a divine wisdom in fasting. Among them is this: that, in the days when He Who is the Dayspring of the Sun of Truth engages, through divine inspiration, in revealing the verses of God, in establishing His religion, and in setting forth His teachings, He is so enraptured and enkindled as to find no time for food or drink. For example, when Moses went up to Mount Sinai to establish the religion of God, He fasted for forty days; and fasting was therefore enjoined upon the Israelites to awaken and admonish them. Likewise Christ, at the beginning of the foundation of His divine religion, the establishment of His teachings, and the formulation of His admonitions, disregarded for forty days all physical necessities and refrained from food and drink. The Apostles and

early Christian believers also fasted, but this fast was changed by the Church Councils to abstinence from certain foods. Similarly, the Qur'án was revealed during the month of Ramaḍán[15] and therefore the fast was enjoined during that period. In the same way, in the beginning of His manifestation, the Báb would be so overcome with emotion at the revelation of the divine verses that for days He would confine himself to drinking tea. Likewise, in the days when He was instituting the divine teachings, and when the divine verses would be sent down continuously, Bahá'u'lláh would be so overwhelmed with the intensity of their influence and the emotions surging within His heart that He would take but little food.

Our meaning is that it has been enjoined upon the generality of the people to fast likewise for a few days, that they might follow the example of the divine Manifestations and call to mind Their state and condition. As history records, the Christians would in the early days observe a complete fast. For every sincere soul who has a beloved aspires to whatever condition his beloved is experiencing: If the beloved were sad he would wish for sorrow, and if joyous he would aspire to joy; if the beloved were at ease he would seek comfort, and if troubled he would desire the same. Now, since in those days the Báb and Bahá'u'lláh would abstain from food and drink, or would partake of only the least amount, it became incumbent upon Their loved ones to follow

3

their example. Even as it is said in the Tablet of Visitation: ". . . who, for love of Thee, have observed all whereunto they were bidden."[16] This is but one of the wisdoms of fasting.

4     The second wisdom is that fasting is conducive to spiritual awareness. One's heart grows more tender, one's spirituality is increased, and as a result one's thoughts become purely focused on the remembrance of God. Such awareness and awakening leads inexorably to spiritual progress.

5     The third wisdom is this. There are two kinds of fast: material and spiritual. The material fast consists in abstaining from food and drink, that is, refraining from satisfying the physical appetites. But the true and spiritual fast is for man to forsake covetous desires, heedlessness, and evil and animalistic attributes. The material fast is therefore a symbol of that spiritual fast. It is like saying: "O Divine Providence! As I am abstaining from bodily desires and from all occupation with food and drink, even so purify and sanctify my heart from the love of anyone save Thyself, and shield and protect my soul from corrupt inclinations and satanic qualities, that my spirit may commune with the breaths of holiness and fast from the mention of all else besides Thee."

# 6

## The Rejection of the Manifestations of God in Every Age[17]

When Abraham was sent forth, however much He expounded the truth, established the religion of God, disseminated new teachings, and explained the divine mysteries, the Assyrians and the Chaldeans would say, "This is but an idle fancy and an empty tale, a mere figment of the imagination. It will never come to pass." Even more, they called it sheer ignorance and counted themselves among the exponents of reason and understanding. But before long it became clear that what Abraham had proclaimed was indeed the truth, and that it was their own thoughts that were the idle fancies. For after a short time the teachings of Abraham were realized in the world: The Holy Land was given to His descendants; the foundations of the religion of God were established; Isaac and Jacob came into the world;

Joseph became ruler in Egypt; Ishmael was blessed and illumined Mount Párán; Moses the Interlocutor appeared, beheld in the desert of Sinai the blazing fire of God in the Burning Bush, rescued the Israelites from their oppression and captivity at the hands of the Egyptians, led them to the Holy Land, and, through His teachings and His religion, which were consonant with the needs of the age, founded a mighty nation. Thus did the deniers fully experience their error, yet they were not chastened or admonished.

2     On the contrary, when Moses appeared they erred anew, for Pharaoh's people regarded the teachings and the law of Moses as mere fancy and accorded them no importance, considering their own ideas to represent the truth. But after a short time it became clear and evident that what Moses had proclaimed was indeed the truth and had come to pass, that the religion of God had been put into full effect and had secured the honor and advancement of all Israel, and that it was the thoughts and imaginations of the Egyptians that were the idle fancies. This was the second experience and yet the people were still not admonished and awakened, but rather persisted in their ignorance until Jesus appeared with a beauteous countenance and an eloquent tongue, and spread abroad the sweet savors of the rose-garden of divine mysteries and imparted the grace of the Holy Spirit.

3     The people, notwithstanding their two previous experiences wherein their error had been established, claimed

again that the teachings of the glorious Gospel were idle fancies—that they were mere thoughts and imaginations, that they were devoid of all reality, and that they lacked in philosophical substance. "These are but vain and idle thoughts," they would say, "whereas we possess true knowledge and lofty ideas, we have wisdom and discernment, and we know the ways of sound governance." But before long their error was exposed, for what Jesus had said was sound and true: It was heavenly thoughts and divine teachings, whereas the prevailing thoughts of the tribes and nations of the earth were the vain and idle fancies. This was the third error and yet another experience which was later also repeated upon the appearance of Muḥammad and the Báb.

Now Bahá'u'lláh has appeared, the divine teachings 4 and admonitions have been unveiled, the call of the oneness of humanity has been sounded, the banner of the kingdom of peace is flying, and the tabernacle of love and harmony amongst all mankind has been raised in the very heart of the world and is summoning all people. And yet again some ignorant souls imagine that these divine teachings are without foundation and regard their own imaginations as lofty thoughts. But before long it will become manifest that what He has proclaimed is sound, proven, and compelling, and that all other thoughts are vain and idle.

# 7

## The Meaning of "Mysteries"[18]

1 Question: What is meant by "mysteries" in the blessed Tablets?

2 Answer: By "mysteries" is meant such matters and questions as are remote and hidden from the minds and understandings of the people, but which can later be grasped by fair-minded souls if a perfect Individual unravels and explains them. Thus, the reality of the advent of Christ was one of God's mysteries in the Mosaic Dispensation, which was later disclosed and witnessed through the manifestation of Christ.

# 8

## The Transformation of Matter across the Kingdoms of Existence

Throughout this endless universe, the greatest  1
means for the progress and renewal of existence is
that all things are eaters and eaten. This is a condition
that applies to all the particles of the universe, and it
is through this means that created things are renewed,
transformed into one another, and endowed with a new
reality unlike the previous one. And this indeed is the
means of renewal.

For instance, in the mineral kingdom the soil absorbs  2
the air and the water and decomposes the creatures
within it, and thus enables the existence of plants. The
more microscopic animals exist in the soil, the better
the plants will grow. And when the plant has grown, it
is consumed by the animal, is incorporated in its body,
and is endowed with a new existence. Thus it progresses

further and assumes a higher reality than that which it initially possessed. This indeed is the means of progress and renewal from the mineral to the vegetable, from the vegetable to the animal, and from the animal to the human world. For as plants grow they are eaten by the animal and replace those elements which have been depleted in the latter's body. In this manner the plants enter the animal kingdom. The microscopic organisms in the air, water, and food enter in turn the body of man and replace that which has been assimilated therein.

3    Thus there is progress in these passages and renewals: The mineral passed from the mineral to the vegetable, then to the animal, and finally to the human realm. And were it not for the cycle of the eater and the eaten, no renewal would take place. Such a renewal, however, is one of the inherent requirements of existence, and all contingent things are bound to pass from one condition to another.

4    The pain and sting of death consists in the dissolution of what was composed and its passage from one condition to another. When one is accustomed to composition, then decomposition is a painful torment; when one is used to a certain degree and station, it is difficult to take leave of it. It is therefore clear that death is merely the passage from one condition to another. Thus if a predatory animal devours another animal, the latter has in reality not been abased but has been decomposed and recomposed, found a renewed existence, and

passed from one body to another. This motion and renewal of beings gives rise to the orderly arrangement and interconnectedness of all things, and were it not for these passages across the vegetable, animal, and human realms, the chain of being would be broken and the innate order of nature would be disrupted.

# 9

## Ṭáhirih and the Conference of Badasht

1     Question: Can you provide an account of Ṭáhirih's deliverance from Qazvín, her arrival in Ṭihrán, her departure for Badasht, and the events that transpired there?

2     Answer: In brief, what happened is the following. Those were the early days of the Cause and no one was informed of the divine teachings. All followed the law of the Qur'án and regarded warfare, retribution, and retaliation as permissible. In Qazvín, Ḥájí Mullá Taqí[19] launched an attack from the pulpit and condemned those two resplendent stars, Shaykh Aḥmad-i-Aḥsá'í and Siyyid Kázim-i-Rashtí. He cursed and reviled them vehemently, saying: "This affair of the Báb, which is unmitigated error, is a hellish fire that has blazed forth from the grave of Shaykh Aḥmad and Siyyid Kázim." In

sum, he uttered the most brazen words and repeatedly hurled insults and invective at them.

A believer from Shíráz[20] was present at his sermon 3 and heard it with his own ears. As he was unaware of the divine teachings that were yet to be promulgated and the principles upon which the religion of God was to be established, he concluded that it behooved him to act according to the law of the Qur'án, and thus he set out to settle the score. He went before dawn to the mosque of the said Ḥájí Mullá Taqí and concealed himself in an alcove. When at dawn Ḥájí Mullá Taqí came to the mosque, that individual stabbed him in the back and in the mouth with a spear-tipped cane. Ḥájí Mullá Taqí fell to the ground and his assailant fled. When the people arrived, they saw the cleric lying dead.

A great tumult erupted and throughout the city a 4 hue and cry was raised. The dignitaries of the town decided in concert that the assassins were Shaykh Rasúl-i-'Arab and two other individuals, whom they viewed as being among the associates of Ṭáhirih. They immediately arrested these three individuals, and Ṭáhirih herself was subjected to severe restrictions. When that man from Shíráz saw that others had been apprehended in his place, he felt it unfit to remain silent and came of his own accord to the seat of the government to declare that Shaykh Rasúl and his friends were entirely innocent of the wrongful accusations levelled against them, and that he himself was the murderer. He described in full detail what had transpired, and confessed, saying: "These people are innocent: Set them free, for I am the guilty one and it is I who must be punished." They arrested him but kept the others captive.

5    Briefly, they brought these four people from Qazvín to Ṭihrán. No matter how much that man from Shíráz protested that it was he who was guilty and that the others were entirely innocent—explaining that he had committed the crime because the victim had openly cursed and reviled his master from the pulpit and that, outraged and unable to contain himself, he had there-fore stabbed him in the mouth with a spearhead—no one listened. To the contrary, Ḥájí Mullá Taqí's son clamored before the ministers of the government for the death of all four. Ṣadru'l-'Ulamá, who was the head of the clergy, sought an audience with the Sháh and said: "Ḥájí Mullá Taqí was an illustrious man, highly renowned in the eyes of all and deeply revered by the people of Qazvín. In avenging the murder of such a man, a single individual is of no consequence. All four men must be turned over to the heirs of Mullá Taqí and delivered to Qazvín, that they may be executed in that city and that its inhabitants may thus be placated." Out of regard for Ṣadru'l-'Ulamá and the people of Qazvín, the Sháh gave word that all four could be executed.

6    The man from Shíráz, seeing that the others had not been released in spite of his own arrest, escaped

on a snowy night and went to the house of Riḍá Khán. Together they made a pact and departed for Shaykh Ṭabarsí, where they both met with martyrdom. As to Shaykh Rasúl and his friends, they were taken to Qazvín, where the populace fell upon them and killed them in the most horrendous manner.

As a result, Ṭáhirih met with the greatest hardship. No one would associate with her, and all her relatives— even her husband and two sons—showed the greatest enmity and would oppress and revile her. Bahá'u'lláh dispatched Áqá Hádíy-i-Qazvíní from Ṭihrán and, by an elaborate stratagem, arranged for Ṭáhirih to be rescued from Qazvín and brought directly to the private quarters of His house. At first no one knew of this, but when some within the inner circle of the believers were informed, they came to see her. I was a child, sitting on her lap and being held in her arms. The curtain was drawn, and those believers were seated in an adjoining room while she was speaking. The purport of her discourse, which was supported by a range of arguments, as well as by the Qur'án and the traditions of the Prophet, was that in every age an illustrious and distinguished Individual must be the focal Center of the circle of guidance, the Pole Star of the firmament of the most excellent Law of God, and a perspicuous Leader; that all may defer to Him; and that in this day that illustrious and distinguished Individual is the Báb, Who has manifested Himself. Although her speech was eloquent, yet when she perceived that Bahá'u'lláh was to raise another call and shine forth with another radiance, she became even more enkindled and reached a state that can hardly be described. She forsook all patience and composure and well-nigh rent asunder the veil of concealment. Night and day she would at turns speak forth and cry out, laugh aloud, and weep bitterly.

8     Later Bahá'u'lláh sent her with a number of believers towards Badasht. Their first stop was a beautiful and verdant garden. Ṭáhirih and the friends arrived there and were later joined by Bahá'u'lláh, Who rested the night there. In the morning He sent Ṭáhirih and the friends with ample provisions to Badasht. After a few days, Bahá'u'lláh Himself went there. When He reached Badasht, Quddús had returned from Khurásán and he, too, came to Badasht, but he remained concealed.

9     In Badasht there was a field with a stream running through it and gardens to either side. Quddús remained concealed in one of the gardens, and Ṭáhirih resided in the other. A tent had been pitched for Bahá'u'lláh on that field, and the other believers were also housed in tents erected on the same field. In the evenings Bahá'u'lláh, Quddús, and Ṭáhirih would meet. Bahá'u'lláh made a solemn agreement with them that the truth of the Cause would be proclaimed at Badasht, but no specific day was designated.

10     Then, by chance, Bahá'u'lláh fell ill. As soon as he was informed, Quddús emerged from his concealment

and entered Bahá'u'lláh's tent. Ṭáhirih sent a message saying: "Either bring Bahá'u'lláh to the garden where I reside or I will come myself." Quddús said: "Bahá'u'lláh is unwell and cannot come," which was a signal. Ṭáhirih, seizing upon the opportunity, arose and, unveiled, came forth from the garden. She proceeded towards the tent of Bahá'u'lláh crying out and proclaiming: "I am the Trumpet-blast; I am the Bugle-call!"—which are two of the signs of the Day of Resurrection mentioned in the Qur'án. Calling out in this fashion, she entered the tent of Bahá'u'lláh. No sooner had she entered than Bahá'u'lláh instructed the believers to recite the Súrih of the Event from the Qur'án, a Súrih that describes the upheaval of the Day of Resurrection.

In such wise was the Day of Resurrection pro- 11 claimed. The believers were seized with such fear and terror that some fled, others remained bewildered and dumbfounded, and still others wept and lamented. Some were so dismayed that they fell ill, and Ḥájí Mullá Ismá'íl was so overcome with fear and terror that he cut his own throat. But after a few days, peace and composure were regained and the confusion and anxiety were dispelled. Most of those who had fled became steadfast again, and the episode of Badasht drew to a close.

# 10

## Shaykh Ahmad and Siyyid Kázim

1    Question: What is the story of Shaykh Ahmad-i-
     Ahsá'í and Siyyid Kázim-i-Rashtí, the journey of
their disciples to Shíráz, and their declaration of allegiance to the Báb, and how did these events unfold?

2    Answer: Know that in the latter days the Shí'ihs of
Persia had forgotten the truth of the religion of God
and had become entirely devoid and deprived of the
morals of the spiritually minded. They were cleaving to
empty husks and remained entirely heedless of the pith
and substance. They had nothing to show but outward
observances, such as prayer, fasting, pilgrimage, alms-
giving, and the commemoration of the blessed Imáms.
The people of true knowledge would therefore call
them "Qishrí" (superficial), for amongst them the inner
truths and meanings were absent, spiritual perceptions

were non-existent, and heavenly morals had become but an idle matter.

When the night of separation approached the dawn— 3 that is, when the concealment of the True One ran its course and the dawn of the morn of God drew nigh— Shaykh Aḥmad-i-Aḥsá'í appeared. He guided the people to inner truths and meanings and expounded the secrets and mysteries of the Qur'án. The Shí'ihs then became divided into two camps: Some followed the august Shaykh and became known as Shaykhís, while others kept to their prior condition and were called "Qishrí."

The illustrious Shaykh began to invite the people to 4 anticipate the advent of God's revelation and the blazing of the Fire of Sinai. He proclaimed, in his writings and in his lessons, that the dawn was fast approaching and that the appearance of the promised Manifestation was imminent. Thus did he seek to instill receptivity in the hearts of the people and admonish them to await day and night the advent of the divine Manifestation. He became most renowned for his knowledge and perfections, not only in Persia but throughout the Shí'ih world. He was mentioned at every gathering and was sought after by all.

During his lifetime he trained and instructed Siyyid 5 Káẓim-i-Rashtí, and before he died he appointed him as his successor. Siyyid Káẓim followed in the footsteps of the illustrious Shaykh and occupied himself night and day with elucidating the inner truths and meanings and in disseminating the secrets and mysteries of the Qur'án. He so imbued the people with anticipation for the coming Revelation that his disciples, in their eagerness, forsook all patience and repose and dispersed in every direction until they found the Promised One.

6     Moreover, Siyyid Kázim explicitly specified, in the preamble of his book "Sharḥ-i-Qaṣídih,"[21] the name of Bahá'u'lláh: "Praise be to God Who hath adorned the preamble of the book of His Essence with the mystery of distinction, the ornament of that Point wherefrom the Há is manifested, with neither assimilation nor separation, through the Alif." To fully explain this expression to you would take a long time, since you are unfamiliar with such words and expressions, and were I to do so it would fill an entire book. But since time is short I will briefly provide a word-for-word translation[22] so that you will understand the general meaning. He says: Praise be to God who has adorned the book of existence with the mystery of distinction through degrees, for it is through such differences that the world of existence is adorned. If all things were of one kind and there were no distinctions, existence would be imperfect. The realm of God and the realm of creation, the realm above and the realm below, the realm of truth and the realm of illusion: All these distinctions are among the inherent requirements of existence. He then says that the book of existence

is adorned with that Point wherefrom the letter Há' appears and the letter Alif is manifested. And in the same book he explains in numerous passages that the Point is the letter Bá'. And when the letters Bá', Há', and Alif are brought together it makes "Bahá."

Siyyid Kázim also spoke of triliterals and quadriliterals. A triliteral is a word comprising three letters, such as "'Alí," and a quadriliteral is a word comprising four, such as "Muḥammad."[23] When these two are combined it makes "'Alí-Muḥammad," which is the blessed name of the Báb. In numerous passages of the same book he explicitly refers to the Báb and extols Him with boundless laudations and attributes, saying that the mysteries of all that has been and all that shall be are found in Him. He also says that all the inner truths and meanings of the Sacred Scriptures are enfolded and allusively expressed in the verse "Bismi'lláhi'r-Raḥmáni'r-Raḥím" (In the name of God, the Merciful, the Compassionate), that all the meanings of "Bismi'lláh" (in the name of God) are encapsulated and comprehended in the letter Bá', which is the sum total of all truths and mysteries, and that the Bá' refers to Bahá'u'lláh.

The late Siyyid had asked the illustrious Shaykh to expound in some way that Hidden Mystery. The Shaykh wrote in reply: "There must needs be a Seat for this Cause and a Place for every Announcement." That is, this Cause upon which we have embarked has a designated Seat and Center, and every Announcement must be established from a given place, meaning a center wherein it is realized. Then he said: "I can say no more; I can appoint no time. 'His Cause will be made known after a while (Ḥín).'"[24] That is, I cannot specify that determined Center and cannot explicitly say Who He is. Then he cites this verse of the Qur'án: "His Cause will be made known after a while (Ḥín)."[25] The preceding verse is "He, verily, is naught but a Remembrance unto all the worlds." In the Commentary on the Súrih of Joseph, the Báb refers to Himself as "the Remembrance of God." The august Shaykh intimates here that that "Seat and Center" is "the Remembrance of God," and that the verse "His Cause will be made known after a while (Ḥín)" means that you will grasp whatsoever that intended Center will announce and proclaim after "Ḥín." Now, according to the *abjad* reckoning, "Ḥín" is equivalent to sixty-eight and "after Ḥín" is sixty-nine, the year of Bahá'u'lláh's revelation.[26] The substance of these words is that whatsoever that Remembrance of God will announce and intimate will become clear and manifest in the year after Ḥín, that is, in the year sixty-nine.

9    As a result of the passionate encouragement of the illustrious Shaykh to anticipate the advent of God and of his assertion of its imminence, and likewise as a result of the utterances of the illustrious Siyyid who night and day proclaimed the approach of that advent—going so far as to instruct his disciples one day to go forth and

seek after their Master—Mullá Ḥusayn and some of the Siyyid's other disciples set themselves to the search. And since a tradition had been reported that the Promised One would go to the mosque of Kúfih, they also went to that mosque and stayed there for a time, awaiting His advent. Even the illustrious Siyyid himself, at the close of his life, left Karbilá for a visit to Káẓimayn and Samarra and returned. In the course of his journey to Samarra, and in the village of Musayyib he spoke to his disciples of his own death. When his disciples began to weep and lament, crying out and beseeching him, he asked them: "Would ye not wish that I pass from this world, that your Master may appear?"

In brief, our meaning is that these two illustrious 10 souls endowed their followers with the greatest receptivity. That is why after the passing of the late Siyyid his disciples sought with all their might after the Promised Beauty. Mullá Ḥusayn and some of his disciples departed from Iraq, made for Persia, and were taken up with the search till they entered the city of Shíráz. As Mullá Ḥusayn had met the Báb before in Karbilá and knew Him, he became His guest. On the night of the fifth of Jamádíyu'l-Avval,[27] Mullá Ḥusayn was seated in the presence of the Báb, who was preparing the tea. As the Báb was serving the tea, He recited certain verses. Mullá Ḥusayn was amazed and astonished to hear a young man, with no religious education or training in the Arabic tongue, recite verses of the utmost eloquence and power, a feat which he could have never thought possible. This led to his awakening and allegiance. The following day he told his disciples and others that he had found the Object of their search and proceeded to describe and portray Him, but he concealed His identity and did not divulge His name. However, he so extolled His attributes that his disciples and the others were enthralled with this news and with unrelenting thirst continued to search for the life-giving waters. Finally, after a few days, he specified His blessed Name. A great commotion ensued. Seventeen people bore allegiance to Him, and the letter of Ṭáhirih, which was with a certain Mírzá Muḥammad-'Alí, was presented to the Báb. For Ṭáhirih had given him this letter and asked him to present it to the Promised One when once they had found Him. In that letter she had included the following ode, the opening of which reads:

> The effulgence of Thy face flashed forth,
> And the rays of Thy visage arose on high.
> Then speak the word, "Am I not your Lord?"
> And "Thou art, Thou art!" we will all reply.[28]

11    Thus Ṭáhirih became the eighteenth believer. The Shí'ihs believed in fourteen immaculate Souls and four Gates. The fourteen immaculate Souls are Muḥammad, Fáṭimih, and the twelve Imáms. The four Gates are the four individuals who succeeded one another as

the leaders of the Shí'ihs after the twelfth Imám. Thus these eighteen souls were appointed to match those eighteen—the main intent was the number. The Báb Himself was the nineteenth. Such is the basis of the number nineteen that has been mentioned in all the Books and Tablets of the Báb. The names of the Letters of the Living are as follows:

1. Mullá Ḥusayn
2. Muḥammad-Ḥasan, his brother
3. Muḥammad-Báqir, his nephew
4. Mullá 'Alíy-i-Basṭámí
5. Mullá Khudá-Bakhsh-i-Qúchání, later named Mullá 'Alí
6. Mullá Ḥasan-i-Bajistání
7. Siyyid Ḥusayn-i-Yazdí
8. Mírzá Muḥammad Rawḍih-Khán
9. Sa'íd-i-Hindí
10. Mullá Maḥmúd-i-Khu'í
11. Mullá Jalíl-i-Urúmí
12. Mullá Muḥammad-i-Ibdál-i-Marághi'í
13. Mullá Báqir-i-Tabrízí
14. Mullá Yúsuf-i-Ardibílí
15. Mírzá Hádí, son of Mullá 'Abdu'l-Vahháb-i-Qazvíní
16. Mírzá Muḥammad-'Alíy-i-Qazvíní
17. Ṭáhirih
18. Quddús

12    The greatness and glory of most of these Letters of the Living resides solely in the fact that they professed their faith at the very beginning. Among them and in terms of importance, a few souls occupy a primary position—Mullá Ḥusayn, Quddús, and Ṭáhirih; a few other blessed souls occupy a secondary position; and the rest are honored solely for having believed in the very beginning—two of them even, like Judas Iscariot, recanted their faith later.

13    After the blessed person of the Báb came to light and His fame spread, Mullá Ḥusayn unloosed his tongue and openly taught the Faith, and was charged to go to other provinces and teach. These in short are the events surrounding the declaration of allegiance of Mullá Ḥusayn and the other Letters of the Living.

# 11

## The Declaration of Bahá'u'lláh

Question: On what date did the dawning of the  1
Sun of Truth and the advent of the Blessed
Beauty take place?

Answer: From the beginning of His childhood  2
Bahá'u'lláh was possessed of such astonishing qualities,
signs, and utterances as to amaze every soul. All the
dignitaries of Persia would say: "This youth is wrought
of a rare substance," and everyone, even the enemies
and the envious, bore witness to His knowledge, grace,
wisdom, understanding, intelligence, and perception.
Among other things, it was acknowledged by all that
He had neither entered a school nor received a religious
education. Nonetheless, His knowledge and perfections
were well recognized. The learned men of Persia would
submit to Him the difficult questions that perplexed
their minds, and He would resolve them. To this day,

and in spite of their hostility, the dignitaries of Persia bear witness to this matter.

3     In sum, no one, whether in Persia or even throughout the East, denies Bahá'u'lláh's knowledge, perfection, greatness, and ability. At most they claim that this Man subverted the foundations of the Law of God, that by means of His shrewdness, intelligence, knowledge, wisdom, eloquence, and sagacity He led astray a vast multitude, and that He thus undermined the perspicuous religion of God. But they do not deny His greatness.

4     Thus, from the very beginning of the Revelation of the Báb, the believers were humble and lowly before Bahá'u'lláh, looked to Him for guidance, and were drawn to Him with a heartfelt attraction. But at Badasht the greatness and majesty of Bahá'u'lláh were manifested to a further degree. There, a number of believers developed a particular devotion and became wholly attracted to Him. Whoever met Him and heard His words would be transformed and enthralled, and could do naught but surrender his will and become aflame with the fire of the love of God.

5     During His final days in Ṭihrán, prior to the journey to Baghdád, some of the believers, such as Muḥammad Taqí Khán, Sulaymán Khán, Jináb-i-'Aẓím, Mírzá 'Alí-Muḥammad, Mullá 'Abdu'l-Fattáḥ, and Mírzá 'Abdu'l-Vahháb—all of whom were to be later martyred—as well as Mírzá Ḥusayn Kirmání and many other souls, perceived that Bahá'u'lláh occupied a transcendent sta-

tion and became convinced that He was a Manifestation of God. Bahá'u'lláh had composed an ode from which the fragrance of a heavenly station could be perceived, the opening of which reads: "'Tis from Our rapture that the clouds of realms above are raining down." All the friends would recite that ode with the utmost fervor and attraction, and all accepted its purport—not a soul voiced an objection. That ode was indeed most enthralling.

The first person who recognized the sublimity and holiness of Bahá'u'lláh and became certain that He would manifest a momentous Cause was Mullá 'Abdu'l-Karím-i-Qazvíní, whom the Báb had named Mírzá Aḥmad. He was the intermediary between the Báb and Bahá'u'lláh and was aware of the truth of the matter.[29]    6

After coming to Baghdád from Persia, Bahá'u'lláh declared to a certain extent the nature of His mission in the ninth year after the appearance of the Báb, and became known among the friends as the appearance of Ḥusayn. For the people of Persia believed that the appearance of the promised Mahdi must be followed by that of Ḥusayn, that is, of Imám Ḥusayn the martyr, to whom they are indeed most attached and bear the greatest allegiance.    7

Now, in all His Books and Scriptures, the Báb heralded that which was to transpire in the year nine. Among them, there abound expressions such as: "In the year nine ye shall attain unto all good." And such state-    8 ments as "In the year nine ye shall . . .", and "Then ye shall . . .", and "Then ye shall . . ." are numerous. Likewise, He says: "Wait thou until nine will have elapsed from the time of the Bayán. Then exclaim: 'Blessed, therefore, be God . . .'" In sum, the tidings of the Báb regarding the year nine are such as to defy all description. Nevertheless certain souls faltered, among them Mírzá Yaḥyá, Siyyid Muḥammad-i-Iṣfahání, and a few others. The Sermon of Salutations (Khuṭbiy-i-Ṣalavát) was revealed in the year nine, and likewise the commentary on the verse of the Qur'án "All food was allowed to the children of Israel except what Israel forbade itself" (Lawḥ-i-Kullu'ṭ-Ṭa'ám) issued forth in that same year.

9    Perceiving the covert rebellion of Mírzá Yaḥyá and others, Bahá'u'lláh journeyed alone to Sulaymáníyyih and was absent for two years. During that time, Mírzá Yaḥyá was acting with utmost caution behind a veil of concealment and, fearing the attention of the General Consul of Persia in Baghdád, disguised himself, took the name of Ḥájí 'Alí, and engaged in selling shoes and plaster in Baṣrah and in Súqu'sh-Shuyúkh in the vicinity of Baghdád. The Cause became entirely quiescent, the Call ceased to be heard, and all name and trace thereof well-nigh vanished.

10    During His sojourn in Sulaymáníyyih, Bahá'u'lláh penned a number of works, among them certain prayers of which copies are still extant, and certain epistles on mystical wayfaring addressed to the doctors and the

learned men of Islam, which are likewise still extant. In those epistles certain teachings are expounded, among them words to this effect: "Were it not contrary to the perspicuous Law of God, I would have given my would-be murderer to be my heir. But what am I to do—I have no worldly possessions, nor hath it been thus decreed by His sovereign will."

In any event, all the doctors and learned men of 11 Sulaymáníyyih attested to the knowledge, attainments, and perfections of Bahá'u'lláh and developed an affection for His person; that is, they would say that this Man was unique and ranked among the chosen ones of God.

When Bahá'u'lláh returned from Sulaymáníyyih, He 12 illumined Baghdád with His light: The call of God was raised anew and a tumult arose in Persia. In Baghdád Bahá'u'lláh stood firm before all peoples. The government of Persia was extremely hostile in those days, and all were seeking by every means to cause Him suffering and to bring Him to harm. At last the Persian government, having grown alarmed at His influence, said: "Baghdád is close to Persia and is a place of passage for the Persians. Thus, in order to put out this fire Bahá'u'lláh must be banished to a distant land." The Persian government then petitioned the Ottoman government, and Bahá'u'lláh was as a result transferred with all due honor out of Baghdád. Leaving the city, Bahá'u'lláh went to the garden of Najíb Páshá and resided there for twelve days. During that time many people, both high and low, and even the Governor and a number of other officials, attained His blessed presence. These are the twelve days of Riḍván.

13    In any event, it was by means of hints and allusions that Bahá'u'lláh first declared His mission during those twelve days. Certain among the friends grasped His intent, but others did not fully understand. At last Bahá'u'lláh came to Constantinople and the Súrih of pilgrimage was revealed, wherein the instruction is given to circumambulate the House of Baghdád. In that Súrih the Cause is openly manifest, but the phrase "He Whom God shall make manifest" does not appear.

14    Subsequently, the Persian government caused Bahá'-u'lláh to be further banished to Adrianople. From there numerous Tablets were revealed day and night to the effect that "Since We have been expelled from our homeland and banished from Baghdád to a remote place, that the fire of the love of God might be quenched, the lamp of guidance extinguished, the banner of God hauled down, and the call of the True One silenced, We have therefore chosen to fully reveal the Cause, manifest the proof, raise the call, and hoist the banner of the Cause of God, that all may see that this persecution, enmity, banishment, and exile has only deepened the influence of the Word of God, that the fame of the Cause has been noised abroad, and that the tidings of the advent of the Kingdom of God have reached unto both East

and West." This universal declaration took place in the year 1280. All the friends, with the exception of Yaḥyá and a few of his followers, became firm and devoted believers, and from Adrianople Tablets would ceaselessly flow to Persia.

This is an account, in summary form, of the Declaration of Baháʾuʾlláh. 15

# 12

## Christ and Bahá'u'lláh

1  Some have asserted that, while mighty signs and marvelous deeds have appeared from Bahá'u'lláh, through which His greatness shines forth as resplendent as the sun, yet the Revelation of Christ is superior to and incommensurate with His.

2  Indeed the signs of greatness in Christ are beyond the ken of mortal mind and the grasp of human imagination. And indeed we are most humble and lowly before His sweet and beauteous countenance, and we love Him with all our heart and soul; nay, should it be called for and should divine confirmations assist us, we would readily lay down our lives for His sake. For we regard Him in the light of true greatness and bear allegiance to His truth. But should attention be drawn to this assertion, we will, in all sincerity and love, reply to their objection in the following manner.

Christ was raised among the people of Israel, who  3
lived under Roman rule. Now, in those days the
Romans were world-renowned for their attainments in
every field of human civilization, and so it would not
be a cause of great wonder if an eloquent utterance or
a novel teaching were to issue from Christ. Bahá'u'lláh,
by contrast, appeared in Persia, where useful sciences
were entirely lacking, except insofar as religious laws
and theological studies were concerned. And thus the
appearance of these divine teachings, of these mighty
and momentous signs, from such an individual and in
such a land, is indeed cause for wonder.

Moreover, the words and verses of Christ, when taken  4
altogether, would comprise at most ten pages, whereas
if the verses of Bahá'u'lláh were gathered together from
beginning to end, they would fill several trunks. Aside
from this, the utterances of Christ in the Gospel are
solely concerned with spiritual admonitions and with
the improvement and rectification of human character,
whereas the Writings of Bahá'u'lláh encompass manifold expressions of wisdom and inner meaning, realities
and sciences, counsels and admonitions, and explanations and exegeses of the Sacred Scriptures of old.

At the time of His ascension, Christ had raised up  5
twelve men and four women. There were to be sure a
few others beside these, but they had not reached the
station of certitude. And among these twelve men, one
became His sworn enemy: Judas Iscariot, who, notwith-

standing his position as the chief of the Apostles, arose
to have Him killed. The most prominent among the
remaining eleven was Peter, and even he failed to stand
firm in the face of trials, since, according to the explicit
text of the Gospel, he thrice denied Christ at the hour
of His martyrdom, to the point of entirely recanting
his faith in the last instance. It was only after the cock
crowed that he was reawakened and made contrite and
repentant. Whereas from the inception of this Cause
to the present day, perhaps close to twenty thousand
men, women, and children have offered up their lives
in the path of God. Many of them, under the threat of
the sword, raised the cry of "Yá Bahá'u'l-Abhá!" Many
were told that, if they publicly recanted their faith, they
would keep both their lives and their possessions, and
yet they answered with the cry of "Yá Bahá'u'l-Abhá!"
Thus, at the time of Bahá'u'lláh's ascension, more than
two hundred thousand souls had taken shelter beneath
His blessed shadow and had attained the station of certitude. The renown of Christ did not even reach, in
His own lifetime, Assyria, Chaldea, Asia Minor, or the
regions of Syria, whereas Bahá'u'lláh's renown, in His
own lifetime, had spread throughout East and West.

6      Christ was not widely known among the people—
most would not recognize Him—and He would travel
from village to village and from wilderness to wilderness; and so it was that when they set out to arrest Him
they knew not where to find Him or how to recognize

142

Him. Judas Iscariot came to them and said: "I will show Him to you." They said: "When we enter that place, how will we know who is Christ?" Judas said: "The one whom I will kiss is Christ." Bahá'u'lláh, however, was standing visibly and openly before His foes, was known to all, and withstood the onslaught of a mighty nation. The enemy arrayed against Christ was the feeble Jewish nation which suffered under Roman rule and which, like the present-day Jews of Tiberias and Safed, was a subjugated people. Bahá'u'lláh's enemies, however, were the adherents of one of the most powerful nations of the world. When Christ was taken before the court, He was asked: "Art thou the King of the Jews?" And He replied in all meekness: "Thou sayest it."[30] But, in the great assemblage of Ṭihrán, the voice of Bahá'u'lláh was raised in address to the highest heaven.[31]

This is the truth of the matter. Consider it and ask 7 the deniers to judge with fairness, to forsake blind prejudice, and to apprehend the truth by inference from the Sacred Scriptures. For instance, were you to tell the Christian clergy today that Christ was not known to the people during His own lifetime, they would be most astonished and deny it—whereas it is explicitly recorded in the Gospel that Judas Iscariot accepted what indeed was a paltry sum to reveal the whereabouts of Christ, and that since none among the crowd could recognize Him, he said that whoever he would kiss was Christ and was to be arrested. And so it came to pass.

# Notes

1. This is 'Abdu'l-Bahá's reply to a letter addressed to Him by the Executive Committee of the Central Organization for a Durable Peace. The Tablet, described by Shoghi Effendi in *God Passes By* as of "far-reaching importance," and dated December 17, 1919, was dispatched to the Committee at The Hague by the hands of a special delegation.

2. The foregoing paragraphs are published in *Selections from the Writings of 'Abdu'l-Bahá* (Wilmette, IL: Bahá'í Publishing, 2010), no. 227.

3. This appended section is published in *Selections from the Writings of 'Abdu'l-Bahá*, no. 1.

4. The English equivalent of this name written in Persian by 'Abdu'l-Bahá is not certain.

5. A Tablet of 'Abdu'l-Bahá chanted by Him, the recording of the latter part of which is played for Bahá'í pilgrims during their visit to the House of the Master in Haifa.

6. The English equivalent of this name written in Persian by 'Abdu'l-Bahá is not certain.

7. Probably the Eleventh Annual Convention of the Bahá'í Temple Unity, held at Hotel McAlpin, New York City, 26–30 April 1919, at which the Tablets of the Divine Plan were unveiled.

8. Qur'án 17:15.

9. Bahá'u'lláh.

NOTES

10. The Báb.

11. Marzieh Gail's translation, published in *Memorials of the Faithful*, pp. 22, 30.

12. Published in Corinne True, *Notes Taken at Acca* (Chicago: Bahá'í Publishing Society, 1907).

13. Ibid.

14. Ibid and *Star of the West*, volume 4, number 18, page 305.

15. See Qur'án 2:185.

16. *Prayers and Meditations by Bahá'u'lláh,* no. 180.

17. Published in Corinne True, *Notes Taken at Acca* (Chicago: Bahá'í Publishing Society, 1907).

18. Ibid.

19. The uncle and father-in-law of Ṭáhirih.

20. Mullá 'Abdu'lláh; see *The Dawn-Breakers*, p. 276.

21. See *God Passes By*, p. 97.

22. That is, from Arabic into Persian.

23. In Arabic, only consonants and long vowels are written, and the word "Muḥammad" is therefore spelled with the letters M, Ḥ, M, and D.

24. See *The Dawn-Breakers*, pp. 17–18, and *God Passes By*, p. 97.

25. Qur'án 38:88.

26. The Islamic year 1269 began on 15 October 1852, the midpoint of Bahá'u'lláh's four-month imprisonment in the Síyáh-Chál. It was in this prison that Bahá'u'lláh received His Prophetic Mission.

27. 23 May 1844.

28. See *The Dawn-Breakers*, pp. 81–82.

29. See ibid., pp. 162–69.

30. Matt. 27:11; Mark 15:2; Luke 23:3.

31. Cf. *The Dawn-Breakers*, pp. 648–49.